SUICIDE BOMBINGS

In an age when the Western world is preoccupied with worries about weapons of mass destruction in terrorist hands, terrorists across many parts of the globe are using a more basic device as a weapon – life itself.

Suicide bombing has become a weapon of choice among terrorist groups because of its lethality and unrivalled ability to cause mayhem and fear, but what is the real driving force behind these attacks? For the first time, *Suicide Bombings* analyses concrete data from The Suicide Terrorism Database at Flinders University, Australia, to explain what motivates the perpetrators. The results serve largely to discredit common wisdom that religion and an impressionable personality are the principal causes, and show rather that a cocktail of motivations fuels these attacks, which include politics, humiliation, revenge, retaliation and altruism.

Suicide Bombings provides a short but incisive insight into this much-publicized form of terrorism, and as such is an informative and engaging resource for students, academics and indeed anyone with an interest in this topic.

Riaz Hassan is Emeritus Professor at Flinders University in Adelaide, Australia, and Global Professor of Social Research and Public Policy at New York University Abu Dhabi. In an academic career spanning over forty years he has conducted research in a number of areas including sociology of housing, sociology of suicide and Muslim societies. He is a fellow of the Academy of the Social Sciences in Australia and a member of the Order of Australia.

SHORTCUTS – *"Little Books on Big Issues"*

Shortcuts is a major new series of concise, accessible introductions to some of the major issues of our times. The series is developed as an A to Z coverage of emergent or new social, cultural and political phenomena. Issues and topics covered range from Google to global finance, from climate change to the new capitalism, from Blogs to the future of books. While the principal focus of ***Shortcuts*** is the relevance of current issues, topics, debates and thinkers to the social sciences and humanities, the books should also appeal to a wider audience seeking guidance on how to engage with today's leading social, political and philosophical debates.

Series Editor: Anthony Elliott is a social theorist, writer and Chair in the Department of Sociology at Flinders University, Australia. He is also Visiting Research Professor in the Department of Sociology at the Open University, UK, and Visiting Professor in the Department of Sociology at University College Dublin, Ireland. His writings have been published in sixteen languages, and he has written widely on, among other topics, identity, globalization, society, celebrity and mobilities.

Titles in the series:

Confronting Climate Change
Constance Lever-Tracy

Feelings
Stephen Frosh

Suicide Bombings
Riaz Hassan

Web 2.0
Sam Han

Global Finance
Robert Holton

Freedom
Nick Stevenson

SHORTCUTS – *"Little Books on Big Issues"*

Series Editor's FOREWORD

The day that aircraft brought down the Twin Towers in New York City – September 11, 2001 – must rank as a critical date in the history of political terror. In *Suicide Bombings*, Riaz Hassan traces transformations in the politics of terror through to its twenty-first century instantiation as the destruction of meaning itself – registered in the rise of the terrifying figure of the suicide bomber, the instigator of a culture of pure death through the deployment of 'life as a weapon'. Hassan, the world's premier sociologist in this area, gives us an excellently lucid account of the global rise of suicide bombing, ranging along the way from the crisis of Islam to numerous ideological currents of religious fundamentalism. Hassan's book is sociologically bold and politically significant; it also serves as a superb shortcut to understanding one of the most important issues of our times.

Anthony Elliott

SUICIDE BOMBINGS

Riaz Hassan

Routledge
Taylor & Francis Group
LONDON AND NEW YORK

First published 2011
by Routledge
2 Park Square, Milton Park, Abingdon, Oxon OX14 4RN

Simultaneously published in the USA and Canada
by Routledge
711 Third Avenue, New York, NY 10017

Routledge is an imprint of the Taylor & Francis Group, an informa business

British Library Cataloguing in Publication Data
A catalogue record for this book is available from the British Library

Library of Congress Cataloging-in-Publication Data
Hassan, Riaz, 1937-
Suicide bombings / by Riaz Hassan.
p. cm.
Includes bibliographical references and index.
ISBN 978-0-415-58886-7 (hbk.) – ISBN 978-0-415-58887-4 (pbk.)
1. Suicide bombings. 2. Terrorism–Psychological aspects. I. Title.
HV6431.H3777 2011
363.325–dc22 2010042852

ISBN: 978-0-415-58886-7 (hbk)
ISBN: 978-0-415-58887-4 (pbk)
ISBN: 978-0-203-82788-8 (ebk)

Typeset in Bembo by
Glyph International

CONTENTS

LIST OF ILLUSTRATIONS

Tables

Figures

ACKNOWLEDGEMENTS

The research for this book was funded by a grant from the Australian Research Council. It would have been impossible to carry out the research without the invaluable support and assistance I received from many people in Australia and around the world. I am indebted to Mr Tariq Parvez, the Director General of the Pakistan Federal Investigation Agency, Mr Muhammad Shoaib Suddle, Director General of the National Police Bureau of Pakistan, and several other counter-terrorism officers who wished not to be identified, for sharing information with me on high-value terrorists in Pakistan and also in Afghanistan. Among other people who shared their valuable time and information with me in Pakistan, I would especially like to thank Mr Rahimullah Yusufzai, Dr Abdul Wahab Yousafzai, Professor Murad Moosa Khan and Mr Hasan Raza Pasha.

I would like to thank Dr N. Jayasekera, Surgeon Rear Admiral, and Rear Admiral Thisara Samarasinghe, Deputy Chief of Staff and Director General of Operations, Sri Lankan Navy, Mr Sisira Mendis, Deputy Inspector General of Police, and several other senior counter-terrorism officials for their assistance in giving me access to research sources and information in Sri Lanka. My understanding of the Sri Lankan situation was deepened by my discussions with a number of Sri Lankan humanitarian NGOs and human rights groups and activists during my visits to the country. Similarly, I benefited from my visit to the Interdisciplinary Centre, Herzliya, Israel, and from my discussions with Dr Ely Karmon, Professor Barry Rubin and Dr Reuven Paz. I am also grateful to Ms Lisa Franke, Mr Hassan Jabareen and Ms Rina Rosenberg for their assistance and advice.

Over the past five years I have benefited from my discussions or communications with numerous scholars around the world. It would not be practical to mention all of them, but I would especially like to acknowledge my thanks to Professor Ian McAllister, Professor Scott Atran, Dr Mia Bloom, Professor Robert Goldney, Professor Adam Graycar, Dr Bruce Hoffman, Ms Rita Katz, Dr John Horgan, Dr Michel Roberts, Dr Basel Saleh, Dr Daya Somasundraram, Professor Ivan Szelenyi, Professor Bryan Turner, Professor Talal Asad and Mr Hussain Haqqani.

I received useful feedback from the seminars delivered at Flinders University, Adelaide; Defence Science and Technology Organization, Australia; Department of the Prime Minister and Cabinet, Canberra; Department of the Attorney General, Canberra; Macquarie University, Sydney; Australian Federal Police; The Menzies Research Centre, Canberra; Islamabad Forum, Pakistan; Sri Lankan Navy; International Centre for Ethnic Studies, Colombo; Wellesley College, Boston; Yale University; Graduate Centre of the City University of New York; University of California Los Angeles. Some of the research was presented as part of the key note addresses at the Pakistan Army's International Conference on Psycho-trauma in Islamabad in 2008, the Second World Congress of Middle East Studies, Amman, Jordan in 2006 and the International Conference organized by the Indonesian Police Foundation in Jakarta in the same year. The comments received from the participants at these seminars and conferences allowed me to refine the interpretations of the data.

The conceptual framework of the book and some of the material in Chapter 4 were first presented to my sociology classes on Death and Suicide at Yale University in 2003 and 2006. I am indebted to my students for their probing comments and questions which allowed me to develop my arguments more fully or to hide their weaknesses. I spent the Michaelmas term of 2007 at Nuffield College, University of Oxford, working with Professor Diego Gambetta. He generously shared not only his database on suicide missions but also many valuable insights from his own work on the subject. I am grateful to him, Professor Peter Hedstrom and other members of the college for their time, valuable comments and hospitality. I would like to thank Professor Richard Fardon, head of the Sociology and Anthropology Department of the School of Oriental and African Studies, University of London for facilitating my access to the

SOAS library resources. I am grateful to Flinders University, the Faculty of Social and Behavioural Sciences and my colleagues in the Department of Sociology for their support.

My research assistant Ms Jessica Sutherland worked tirelessly and with admirable commitment and dedication to compile the Flinders University Suicide Terrorism Database (FUSTD), now one of the most comprehensive databases on suicide bombings in the world. The fruits of her efforts are reflected throughout the book. My deepest and warmest gratitude goes to her for her support, assistance and dedication to the project – often under difficult conditions – which played a critical and vital role in achieving the research objectives. Mrs Carolyn Corkindale deserves my sincere thanks for her support and assistance. Sincere thanks also to Ms Elizabeth Blumer for her editorial assistance and to Jennifer Dodd for her support. I want to thank Professor Anthony Elliott, the commissioning editor of the series, for his interest and warm support of the book, and Routledge's Gerhard Boomgaarden, whose enthusiasm for the book matched my own. Finally, my wife, Selva, has helped me in more ways than I can say. Her encouragement and support were vital in the completion of the book. Of course none of the people mentioned is in any way responsible for any shortcomings; for all those I accept full and sole responsibility. This book includes the material which has appeared in my book *Life as a Weapon: The Global Rise of Suicide Bombings* and is dedicated to the victims of all forms of terrorism around the world.

Riaz Hassan
Flinders University and
New York University Abu Dhabi

1

LIFE AS A WEAPON

Historical roots of a modern phenomenon

In an age when the Western world is preoccupied with fears about weapons of mass destruction in terrorist hands, in many parts of the world terrorist groups are turning to a more basic device as their weapon of choice – life itself. The use of life as a weapon – or suicide bombing – has become a weapon of choice among many terrorist groups because of its lethality and ability to cause mayhem and fear. Several prominent past and present leaders of Western democracies have often responded to the phenomenon by describing it as a manifestation of Islamic fanaticism explicable only by the irrationality of those who carry out the suicide attacks. The mass media, taking cues from such explanations, has reinforced this characterization by stereotyping the perpetrators as psychologically impaired and morally deficient, uneducated and impoverished individuals.

Such assumptions have fuelled the belief that acts of suicide terrorism such as the 9/11-type of attacks can be prevented only through the liberalization and democratization of Muslim societies. This was a key rationale used by the United States, the United Kingdom and their allies to garner public support for the wars in Iraq and Afghanistan. Ironically, policies based on such assumptions are reinforcing irrational fears and fostering the development of foreign and domestic policies which are worsening the situation. Externally imposed policies of liberation, liberalization and democratization are likely to sharpen religious and ideological divisions in the world, especially in the recipient Muslim countries. The wars in Iraq, Afghanistan and Pakistan are obvious examples and we can easily add more countries to the list.

Studies by serious scholars show that suicide bombing attacks are linked more to politics than to religion. Religion is used effectively by a number of Islamic radical groups to recruit suicide bombers and to raise operational funds, but the leadership of these groups have secular goals, such as the expulsion of occupying forces from the 'homeland'. Thus, even if some suicide bombers are irrational or fanatical, the leadership of the groups that recruit and direct them is not. Studies that have tried to explain the motivations of suicide attackers in terms of religious fanaticism have tended to focus on the attackers' psychopathology, poverty and lack of education, or individual motives, such as religious indoctrination, especially Islamic fundamentalism (Paz 2002; Lester, Yang and Lindsay 2004; Kramer 1991; Berko 2007; Ganor 2002). These explanations have been found to be seriously flawed.

A number of seminal studies have found that suicide terrorism is not caused by individual psychopathology, poverty or lack of education and that the role of the actual terrorist groups in the indoctrination may be overstated as many volunteers for suicide bombings do not undergo extensive training. The decision to participate in a suicide bombing is facilitated by bombers' internalized social identities, their exposure to asymmetric conflict – in other words, conflict between sides of unequal powers – and to the organizations which sponsor or orchestrate such attacks, as well as by their membership of a larger community in which sacrifice and martyrdom have high symbolic significance. After reaching the decision to carry out an operation, suicide bombers become extremely focused on committing the act. Both the organizations and individuals who engage in suicide terrorism are rational in terms of trying to meet instrumental goals and acting on their values (Atran 2003, 2010; Argo 2004; Bloom 2005; Pape 2005; Gambetta 2005; Crenshaw 2002; Merari 2005a; Silke 2003; Sageman 2004; Post, Sprinzak and Denny 2003).

Other studies have also emphasised that there is little evidence that supporters of suicide terrorism hate democratic freedoms, although they do tend to hate US foreign policy. Lack of civil liberties and US support for regimes that withhold them are related to the attacks on the USA.

An important factor explaining the rise of suicide bombing attacks is the presence of recruiting organizations which use various means to encourage loyalty to the cause and comrades. For the organization itself, the tactic of suicide terrorism is rational, encourages retaliation on the part of the enemy and is successful in achieving its near-term goal of avenging the experience of humiliation – often resulting in broader societal support for the group's cause. It boosts members' morale and demonstrates a desperate situation to the international community.

In societies based on the regulation of public and private behaviour through cultural codes of honour and shame, living under humiliating and demeaning conditions is no better than dying. Suicide attacks are attractive because they result in high levels of damage, are successful in reaching targets, are hard to deter, are cost-effective in terms of reaching their targets, do not require an exit strategy on the part of the attacker, do not leave perpetrators open to interrogation and attract media attention.

A modern phenomenon with ancient roots

Understanding the dynamics of suicide bombings requires an understanding of what drives humans to suicide. According to psychologists, motivations for suicide are accentuated when two fundamental human needs – the need for conformity and social power and the need to belong with or feel connected to significant others – are frustrated. Fulfilment of these needs makes people feel effective and empowered in their social groups (Joiner 2006; Atran 2003; Silke 2006). In modern psychiatry and sociology, suicide is generally regarded as an *end* – an exit from intolerable personal pain and adverse social conditions. In my studies of suicide over the past forty years, however, I have questioned this characterization or description. Suicidal behaviour in a variety of settings may be used *not as an end in itself, but as a means to achieve multiple ends*, including self-empowerment in the face of powerlessness, redemption in the face of damnation and honour in the face of humiliation (R. Hassan 1985, 1995). This is central to a more meaningful understanding and explanation of contemporary suicide bombings in the Middle East, Afghanistan, Sri Lanka and elsewhere. History offers some compelling examples of the use of suicide as a proactive and empowering political act and not as a resolution of personal crisis. I have chosen the following to illustrate this point: the suicide of Roman soldier and statesman Cato; the crucifixion death of Jesus Christ; the Martyrs of Cordoba; the Jewish Zealots and Sicarri; the Ismaillis-Nazari Assassins; and Japanese kamikaze pilots.

Cato's suicide

In the waning years of the Roman republic, Cato had emerged as the most determined and incorruptible opponent of Julius Caesar. Cato became a leader of resistance in the civil war that followed Caesar's rise as dictator. Caesar had defeated one republican army after another on the battlefield. In his victories, he had become magnanimous towards his defeated opponents and had planned the same for Cato after the republican army had been defeated in Africa. But in Caesar's clemency Cato saw a new Rome where all sides, victorious and defeated, would be in Caesar's debt. For Cato, it was an utter defeat of the cause for which he had fought and the complete end of resistance to Caesar's rule.

In his determination to fight this seemingly inevitable outcome, Cato wanted to send a powerful message to the Roman world. As refugees fled in advance of Caesar's arrival, he retired to his chamber to read the *Phaedo* – the famous dialogue in which Socrates, on the day he is to drink poison, discusses the immortality of the soul. Towards dawn, Cato stabbed himself, and when his attendants tried to save him, he pulled open his wounds savagely until he collapsed dead. It was a horrific death and a powerful political message, not only to Caesar, but also to the surviving republican forces and to Rome. 'Cato, I grudge your death as you have grudged my power to keep you alive', was Caesar's response when he arrived at the scene.

Cato's defiant suicide acted as a rallying call for further resistance to Caesar's rule. Within two years of Cato's death, Caesar had been assassinated by his followers. Cato's suicide could not protect the republic, but it succeeded in destroying his enemy. It was not a suicide to escape retribution but rather it reflected a desire for a political impact that Cato felt his continued life could not have (Holland 2003; Silke 2007b; Minois 1999).

The crucifixion death of Jesus Christ

Another historical example supporting my thesis that suicide might not be an end but a means to achieve multiple ends is the crucifixion of Christ.

Was Christ's death a suicide mission? In his gospel, the apostle John quotes Jesus as saying, 'For these sheep I will give my life', and, 'No one takes it from me; I lay it down freely myself' (John 10.15 and 10.18). When Jesus entered Jerusalem for Passover he knew what awaited him; he deliberately moved towards death and during his trial did nothing to avoid it. In the context of divine redemption, Jesus' suicide has a totally different significance and a totally different dimension from ordinary suicide, but the ambiguity remains (Minois 1999: 24).

Christians are enjoined to follow Jesus as an exemplar in all things, including salvation and redemption. They are invited to sacrifice their own lives in the service of a higher cause, and in doing so they can invoke Jesus' pronouncements, such as: 'Whoever would save his life will lose it, but whoever loses his life for my sake will find it' (Matthew 16.25); 'The man who loves his life loses it, while the man who hates his life in this world preserves it to life eternal' (John 12.25); 'There is no greater love than this; to lay down one's life for one's friends' (John 15.13).

The first generations of Christians understood these and similar injunctions, and during the period of persecutions they took them literally, willingly giving themselves over to martyrdom. Writing in the late first century, John tells us that 'the spirits of those who had been beheaded for witness to Jesus and the word of God' (Revelation 20.4) would find places in heaven. In his Apology, written in the second century, St Justin praised Christians who seek death, and in the early third century Tertullian and the Montanists advocated voluntary martyrdom. The Acts of the Christian martyrs abound in examples of Christians who turned themselves over to the civil authorities or who, by their actions and responses to interrogation, deliberately chose death (Minois 1999: 25). One of the best historical examples of this is the 'Martyrs of Cordoba' in ninth-century Spain.

The Martyrs of Cordoba

Almost a hundred years after the Ummayad prince Abd al-Rahman had established the Islamic emirate, the old Visigothic city of Cordoba had been transformed visually, socially and culturally. Cordoba was all bustle, a prosperous boomtown, new construction of every sort everywhere, its peoples, cultures and languages reshuffling themselves along with the changing landscape. A memorable description of this change was captured by Paul Alvarus, an erudite and widely respected Christian luminary of Cordoba, in his famous polemical book, *The Unmistakable Sign*:

> The Christians love to read the poems and romances of the Arabs; they study the Arab theologians and philosophers, not to refute them but to form a correct and elegant Arabic. Where is the layman who now reads the Latin commentaries on the Holy Scriptures, or who studies the Gospels, prophets or apostles? Alas! All talented young Christians read and study with enthusiasm the Arabic books; they gather immense libraries at great expense; they despise the Christian literature as unworthy of attention. They have forgotten their own language. For every one who can write a letter in Latin to a friend, there are a thousand who can express themselves in Arabic with elegance, and write better poems in this language than the Arabs themselves.
>
> *(Menocal 2002: 66)*

Although he himself was a layman, Alvarus shared his horror at the spectacle of a world transformed with a small but highly visible group of conservative Christians. By the middle of the ninth century in Cordoba, the Church had successfully come to terms with the Islamic polity within which it existed. The Islamic government had grown stronger and the cultural life of the court had become vibrant. The Cordovan Christians were increasingly drawn to Islamic culture and the rate of conversions to Islam had accelerated, leading to changes and disruptions at every level of Cordovan society. Society itself had genuinely become tolerant and pluralistic in ways that may be appealing to modern sensibilities but was not to Christian conservatives of the time (Menocal 2002; Coope 1995; Daniel 1979).

Indeed, these changes were deeply alarming for some Cordovan Christians. They feared diversity and despised anyone who did not conform to their beliefs. They believed Muslims had no right to exist and depicted them only through the most hateful of stereotypes. As a symbol of the Christian resistance to assimilation between AD 850 and 859, a radical Christian group led by the Cordovan priest Eulogius and his friend Paul Alvarus launched a martyrdom movement, a course of action which led to the execution of around fifty Christians by the Muslim government of Cordoba. The supporters of the movement were mainly clerics and some laypeople from Cordovan monasteries and basilicas.

One by one, they indulged in conspicuous public declaration of the deceits of Islam and the perfidies of its Prophet. Some appeared before the Muslim *qadi* (high judge) of Cordoba, proclaiming that Muhammad was a magician, an adulterer and a liar and that his followers would certainly go to hell. Others made similar remarks on the streets of Cordoba. Islamic rulers were tolerant in matters of doctrine but not of disparagement of the Prophet Muhammad. The would-be martyrs knew for certain that they were forcing the hands of the authorities of Cordoba by expressly choosing to vilify Muhammad. Leaders on both sides made every attempt to head off their actions and their fatal consequences – in vain. These virulent, blasphemous public attacks thus deliberately invited execution, and close to fifty offending Christians, including Eulogius, were beheaded in public.

The rationale of this martyrs' movement provided by Eulogius was to assert publicly the superiority of the Christian faith as well as the deceits and falsehood of Islam and its Prophet. Eulogius and the other martyrs knew what the punishment for their repeated blasphemies would be, but they believed such actions would not only assert the superiority of their faith but also lead to their salvation. The martyrs' supporters understood the movement as a reaction to the horrors of Muslim rule, a radical but justifiable form of protest. In their writings they compared those executed to the early Roman martyrs. The facts, however, did not fully support such a comparison. The Cordovan martyrs brought about their own arrest and execution; the authorities did not seek them out. As to whether the Muslims in Cordoba actively persecuted Christians, they did so only after the martyrdoms began, not before; thus the martyrs' movement was more likely the cause of ill treatment than a response to it (Colbert 1962; Christys 2002; Makki 1992).

The Cordovan martyrs had expected their actions to lead to widespread civil unrest by both Muslims and Christians, but that did not eventuate. In due course, the passion of the moment passed and life returned to thriving religious coexistence as before. But their martyrdom was not forgotten: they were eventually transformed from a thorn in the side of the Church into the 'Mozarab martyrs' and became the near-sainted symbols of a cause that served the purpose of Christian chroniclers and analysts of later periods as an easy enough touchstone: brave Christians resisting the forced conversion 'by the sword' that conventional history tells us was the way by which Islam spread and suffering death for their heroism (Menocal 2002: 70–72; Coope 1995).

The Jewish Zealots and Sicarii

In the first century AD, the Jewish sects of Zealots and Sicarii were active in stirring up rebellion against the Roman rulers of Jerusalem. They derived their inspiration from the ancient Jewish religious tradition of *herem* – holy war – against the Canaanites and other gentiles for the control of the Promised Land. The name Sicarii is derived from the dagger (*sica*) they used to carry out their terror missions. There is scant reliable information about their activities, but generally Sicarii targeted the Hellenised Jews, who collaborated with the Romans, in order to punish them for their immorality and to send a message that Romans could not protect the Jewish collaborators. The Zealots, meanwhile, targeted the enemy occupiers directly. Both groups adopted a strategy of violent attacks designed to achieve three main goals: to cleanse Judea of foreign influences and bring about messianic redemption; to incite rebellion among the Jews against the Roman occupation; and to prevent any possible reconciliation between the moderate Jews and the Romans (Bloom 2005; Pape 2005).

Members of these sects numbered in the hundreds and, starting around AD 48, carried out suicidal missions to kill prominent Jews, temple priests who had succumbed to Hellenistic culture and Roman soldiers. Their atrocities destroyed any prospect of a mutually agreeable solution and steadily expanded the conflict. According to Rapoport:

> The Zealots saw themselves as revolutionary catalysts who moved men by force of their audacious action, exploiting mass expectations that messianic deliverance was imminent. To generate a mass uprising, they escalated the struggle by shock tactics to manipulate fear, outrage, sympathy and guilt. Sometimes these emotional effects were provoked by terrorist atrocities which went beyond the consensual norms governing violence; at other times, they were produced by provoking the enemy into committing atrocities against his will.
>
> *(Rapoport 1984: 670).*

Zealots and Sicarii continued their attacks for a quarter of a century, provoking brutal Roman retaliatory reprisals. Their attacks succeeded in generating two large-scale uprisings that served as the trigger of the Jewish War of AD 66. This lasted for four years and ultimately led to the destruction of the second Temple in Jerusalem and the massacre of Jews in Egypt and Cyprus, as well as triggering a traumatic exodus of the Jews from Judea. The Jewish War finally ended at Masada. When the Roman army attacked this fortress at the end of AD 72, there were 960 insurgents and refugees within. Once the fall of the fortress became inevitable, Eleazar, the leader of the Zealots, persuaded Masada's defenders to engage in what remains one of the most famous group suicides in history. The Zealots in Masada preferred to die by their own hand rather than be captured by their Roman enemies. The symbolic act demonstrated their steadfast opposition to Roman oppression. The act of mass suicide was a political act. The Zealot leader Eleazar is said to have told his followers as the Roman army were preparing to launch their final assault that God has commanded them:

> ... to be able to die nobly and freely ... Only our shared death is able to protect our wives and children from violation and slavery ... *We*, who have been brought up at home in this way, should set an example to others in our readiness to die ... This – suicide – is commanded by our laws. Our wives and children ask for it. God himself has sent us the necessity for it.
>
> *(Pape 2005: 34).*

The order of Assassins

From 1090 to 1256, a small, secretive Shia Muslim sect in north-western Iran, known as Ismaillis-Nazari, created an effective organization for the planned and systematic use of political terror that relied on self-destruction for success. The sect's name is derived from the Arabic word *hasshishiyyin* because its members reputedly smoked hashish before going on their missions. This was, however, a misconception, but their legacy lives on through the word *assassin*, still used to describe a political murderer. For almost two centuries the Assassins' daggers terrorized and demoralized the mainly Sunni rulers of the region. Their goal was to purify Islam by returning the Umma (Islamic community of believers) to one single community, as had been the case under the first four caliphs of Islam in the seventh century. The Assassins carried out their missions through a network of secret cells in sympathetic neighbouring urban centres. They were highly trained and disciplined killers and used clever strategies to gain access to their victims. Most of their victims were high-status public or military leaders who were so heavily guarded that even successful attackers would almost surely have to pay for their success with their lives. The attacks took place at venerated holy sites, on Muslim holy days and at the royal court when many witnesses were present. The assassinations were a form of communication to the witnessing public of the error of the ways and beliefs of their victims. What made the Assassins so lethal was that they were willing to die to accomplish their missions and often, rather than attempting to escape, revelled in their impending deaths in order to demonstrate the purity of their motives and to enter heaven. It was considered shameful to survive a mission (Pape 2005; Bloom 2005; Hudson 1999; Lewis 1987).

Japanese traditions of political and military sacrifice

Japanese culture offers highly instructive examples of voluntary political suicide. The Japanese samurai could commit two types of *seppuku* (ritual suicide) – *setsujoku* and *kanshi* – for a variety of motives. In *setsujoku*, the motive was to avoid the disgrace of being captured by the enemy. The motive for *kanshi* was entirely political, this being a form of suicide carried out in protest at the action of a superior considered by the samurai to be a grave mistake and also in order to influence political decisions and policy. The case of Takamori Saigo in the nineteenth century has interesting parallels with that of Cato. Following the collapse of the old Shogunal system in Japan with the Meiji Restoration, Takamori Saigo became profoundly disillusioned with the direction taken by the Japanese government. He was a strong supporter of the emperor and thus favoured the Restoration, but viewed the new government as corrupt and indolent.

Saigo led 15,000 samurai in rebellion against Japan's new conscript army, which had been trained and equipped in Western style. At the battle of Shiroyama in 1877, the samurai were crushed by the conscripts. Saigo committed *seppuku* on the battlefield but, as with Cato, his ideology was quickly adopted by the conscript forces that defeated him. Thus, in defeat, Saigo won a great victory for those virtues of which he had feared the loss and which he had sought to defend. Suicide gave Saigo's ideology a potency that allowed it ultimately to prevail (O'Neill 1999).

The second example, the Japanese kamikaze suicide missions in World War II, is more widely known. Sacrifice is part of military heroism, and in World War II it was given vivid imagery and meaning by the Japanese. Desperate to stop the advancing US naval fleet in the Pacific, in July 1944 the Japanese high command in the Philippines began the organization of a variety of 'special attack' air force units whose pilots agreed to crash their planes, gliders and even torpedos into US naval vessels. These units were given the name of Shinpu Special Attacks Corps. The characters for *shinpu* ('divine wind') can also be read 'kamikaze', as they were by Japanese–American translators operating with the Allied fleet, with the result that this is the name by which the world now knows them.

Kamikaze raids operated for ten months, from 25 October 1944 until Japan surrendered on 15 August 1945. In all, some 3,843 pilots gave their lives. Most were young, fairly well-educated men who understood that pursuing conventional warfare would likely end in defeat. These suicide attacks did not stop the Americans, but they were four to five times more deadly than conventional strike missions and imposed high costs on the invasion forces. In the battle of Okinawa (April 1945), 200 kamikaze rammed fully-fuelled fighter planes into more than 300 ships, killing 5,000 Americans in the most costly naval battle in US history (Atran 2003; Pape 2005; Hill 2005).

In total, at least 375 naval vessels were damaged or sunk, 12,300 US servicemen killed and another 36,400 wounded. The kamikaze were enshrined at Yasukuni Jinjo temple and thereby became national gods. They were lionized in the press and official communiqués in which they were referred to as god-heroes. Kamikaze pilots were posthumously awarded a two-rank promotion which entitled their families to increased pension rights and better rations, very important in war time. The families received the title of *homare no ie* ('a household of honour') and were given places of honour at official ceremonies (Larteguy 1956: 128).

Japanese officials rejected the assertion that kamikaze pilots committed suicide, a stance illustrated by the comments of Lieutenant General Torashira Kawabe to Allied interrogators after World War II:

> We believe that our spiritual convictions and moral strength could balance your material and scientific advantages. We did not consider

> our attacks to be 'suicide'. The pilot did not start out on his mission with the intention of committing suicide. He looked upon himself as a human bomb which would destroy a certain part of the fleet ... [and] died happy in the conviction that his death was a step towards the final victory.
>
> *(O'Neill 1999:130–31).*

However, while the kamikaze pilots have been seen as fanatically devoted to the cause, there were detractors amongst them who did not support the strategy but went along with it because they felt *guilty* for not participating when others were sacrificing themselves. They undertook special attack missions and sacrificed themselves out of their sense of *solidarity*, a factor that was repeatedly stressed in their training (Kozu 2000: 316; Oknuki-Tierney 2002: 169).

*

The above cases are illustrations of my thesis that, under certain circumstances, the act of deliberate self-destruction – suicide – is a *means* of achieving multiple *ends*. They show the instrumental use of life itself as a weapon. These ends may include the realization of ideals valued by the actors, or those who are undertaking these actions. The notion of 'weapon' here implies the instrumental use of life as a means to communicate these ideals to the wider community and to inflict physical or symbolic pain and loss on the opponent. In all of these cases, as is also true in the case of suicide bombing in modern times, the actions of the actors are seen by their reference group as rational and altruistic. In this respect, these deeds belong to a family of actions in human society that include religious martyrdom, self-immolation, hunger strikes and war heroism – actions in which people go to extremes of self-sacrifice in the belief that, by doing so, they are furthering the interests of their reference group or the cause they strongly identify with and value.

In French sociologist Emile Durkheim's typology of suicide, such actions would fall in the altruistic category: they are different from other suicidal actions caused by individual motives, personal catastrophes, hopelessness and psychopathologies that lead people to consider life as not worth living (Durkheim 1951). Altruistic actions, in contrast, involve valuing one's life less than one does a group's honour, religion, principles or some other collective interest. Altruism, generally seen as 'doing good', is not antithetical to aggression. In warfare, soldiers risk their lives to help kin, comrades and country and also by killing enemies. It may be puzzling and unsettling but, as shown by the above examples (and many more similar examples that can be extracted from history's pages), a human being's disposition to sacrifice oneself for the benefit and good of the group is an enduring behavioural feature that can manifest itself in a range of material, cultural and organizational settings. Modern suicide bombings fall into this conceptual map (Gambetta 2005; Leenars 2004).

There is another narrative, that of human destiny, which reflects on the nature of a phenomenon like suicide bombing. In this narrative, humanity's lot is one of intertwined pain and frustration, humiliation, injustice, emotional distress, unmerited defeat, interwoven hope and disappointment, and the scorn of the great and the powerful. It is beautifully captured in Hamlet's soliloquy by William Shakespeare:

> To be, or not to be: that is the question:
> Whether 'tis nobler in the mind to suffer
> The slings and arrows of outrageous fortune,
> Or to take arms against a sea of troubles,
> And by opposing end them? To die: to sleep;
> No more; and by a sleep to say we end
> The heart-ache and the thousand natural shocks
> That flesh is heir to. 'Tis a consummation
> Devoutly to be wish'd. To die, to sleep;
> To sleep: perchance to dream: ay, there's the rub;
> For in that sleep of death what dreams may come,
> When we have shuffled off this mortal coil,
> Must give us pause; there's the respect
> That makes calamity of so long life;
> For who would bear the whips and scorns of time,
> The oppressor's wrong, the proud man's contumely,
> The pangs of despised love, the law's delay,
> The insolence of office, and the spurns
> That patient merit of the unworthy takes,
> When he himself might his quietus make
> With a bare bodkin?

(Hamlet, *act 3, scene 1*)

Outline of the book

This book is about a modern expression of the use of life as a weapon for altruistic purposes: suicide bombing. As mentioned earlier, altruistic actions involve valuing one's life less than one does a group's honour, religion or other collective interests. Furthermore, altruistic actions are not necessarily antithetical to aggression. Suicide bombings have increased dramatically over the past three decades. In the modern era, this phenomenon began in Lebanon in the 1980s. It then spread to conflicts in Sri Lanka, Palestine, Chechnya, Turkey and Kashmir before becoming a focus of international attention after the devastating attacks of 11 September 2001 in the USA that shocked the world. Since the US-led invasions of Afghanistan in 2001 and Iraq in 2003, incidents of suicide bombings have surged to extraordinary levels and are rapidly spreading around the world. The impact of the Iraq War alone on the occurrence of suicide bombings can be understood from the fact that since 2003 there have been more suicide bombings in Iraq alone than there were across the whole world in the preceding twenty-five years.

This study deals with the global rise of suicide bombings and the causes behind it. The following chapter provides an overview of the global trends in suicide bombings between 1980 and 2006 based on the analysis of the Flinders University Suicide Terrorism Database, now the most comprehensive database on suicide bombings in the world. It will also offer an analysis of the destructive impact of suicide bombings compared with other forms of terrorism and of the types and targets of suicide bombings. Chapter 3 goes on to give an overview of the main explanatory models accounting for their occurrence and dramatic increase. It will explore the role of humiliation, revenge and altruism at organizational and individual levels in shaping the sub-culture that aids suicide bombings. Chapter 4 will examine the question of whether suicide bombing constitutes homicidal killing or is a weapon of war, as well as why certain types of deaths are regarded as 'good deaths' while others are seen as 'bad' and are stigmatized. The final chapter will be devoted to examining the main lessons about suicide bombings. It will argue that the causes of suicide bombings lie not in individual psychopathology but in broader societal conditions and that therefore suicide attacks are likely to emerge under certain social circumstances. Understanding and knowledge of these conditions is vital for developing appropriate policies and responses in order to protect the public and counter the scourge of suicide bombings.

2

THE GLOBAL RISE OF SUICIDE BOMBINGS

Analysis of trends

The Flinders University Suicide Terrorism Project

The Flinders University Suicide Terrorism Project was established in 2005 through a grant from the Australian Research Council. A key objective of the research project was to construct a global database of suicide bombings between 1981 and 2006, using primary and secondary data. The secondary data involved a census of all suicide bombing attacks during this period. The primary data were to be gathered by interviewing leaders and members of the terrorist organizations which use suicide bombings as a weapon (such as Tamil Tigers, Hezbollah, Hamas, Taliban, Al Qaeda and Laskar-e-Toiba) and supplemented by interviews with survivors, families, recruiters and trainers of suicide bombers.

However, following the enactment of Australia's counter-terrorism laws in 2005, it became a criminal offence under Australian law for Australian citizens to have any contact with a proscribed terrorist organization. On the advice of the Australian authorities, I was obliged to revise the research design and abandon interviews with the leaders of the terrorist organizations, suicide bombers, their recruits, trainers, families and survivors. The new strategy involved interviewing counter-terrorism officials and journalists in some of the major sites of suicide bombings. For logistical reasons (time, expense, permissions and access to these people) this strategy could only be partially followed and produced only limited amounts of information that could be regarded as primary or reliable.

This development had a serious impact on the original objectives of the study. I was forced to revise the study, which meant building the suicide bombing database as I had originally envisaged and largely relying on it for my investigation and analysis of the research issues. This was a big setback as I had hoped that the primary interview material would allow me to explore rigorously not only the political dimension of the act of suicide bombing but, equally importantly, the ideas and motivations for the act of suicide on the part of the sponsoring organizations as well as the individual perpetrators. As signalled in Chapter 1, a key objective of this study was to explore the expression(s) of altruism, if any, in the act of self-destruction by the perpetrators of suicide attacks. Several studies routinely report claims of the leaders of the sponsoring organizations and individual perpetrators that they were acting for altruistic reasons but without solid evidence to back up such claims. This issue would still be explored but not as comprehensively as originally envisaged.

My inability to pursue the research project as originally planned also had obvious implications for 'academic freedom' as it prevented me from pursuing a *bona fide,* publicly funded academic research project. The government stance over the research became a subject of national and international attention (Bonner 2006; Shepherd 2006; Edwards and Stewart 2006; O'Neill 2006; Healy 2008). It also became one of the first concrete examples of how Australia's counter-terrorism laws were limiting academic research (MacDonald and Williams 2007).

Methodology for the development of the Database

The work on the Flinders University Suicide Terrorism Database (FUSTD) began in late 2005 and was completed by the end of 2007, but the work on refining it continued throughout 2008. The following sections will provide an overview of the methodology used to construct the FUSTD and an analysis of suicide bombing attacks between 1981 and 2006, their geographical distribution, relative lethality and targets.

Defining suicide bombing: Difficulties in defining suicide bombing are inextricably related to the data on the subject. Contemporary studies and commentaries on suicide bombing do not offer a concise or even a commonly agreed definition of the concept. More often than not, authors use definitions that highlight a certain feature of the act that emphasizes the focus of their respective study and analysis. For example, Diego Gambetta and contributors to his edited volume use the term 'suicide mission' in order to extend the scope and coverage of their analysis (Gambetta 2005). Mia Bloom, Mohammad Hafez, Robert Pape, Ami Pedahzur and Shaul Shay explicitly use the term 'suicide terrorism' but with a nuance that emphasizes one or more motivational attributes central to their analysis (Bloom 2005; Hafez 2006, 2007b; Pape 2005; Pedahzur 2005; Shay 2004). In the case of these authors, this tends to be on political resistance and altruism. They all use the terms 'suicide bombing', 'suicide terrorism' and 'suicide attacks' interchangeably.

Others, like Raphael Israeli, insist that the term 'suicide terrorism' be used only to describe the violence of Muslim suicide bombers, implying that relatively neutral terms such as 'suicide bomber' are too weak and insufficiently condemnatory (Israeli 1997, 2003). He, along with Anat Berko, Anne Marie Oliver and Paul Steinberg, and Michael Walzer, sees suicide bombings as homicidal killing (Berko 2007; Oliver and Steinberg 2005; Walzer 2004). At the other end of the spectrum, Farhad Khosrokhavar, Nasra Hassan, Talal Asad, Ivan Strenski, Scott Atran and Mohammad Hafez use the term 'suicide bombing' interchangeably with the altruistically coded terms 'martyrdom' and 'sacrifice' (Khosrokhavar 2005; N. Hassan 2001; Asad 2007; Strenski 2003; Atran 2003, 2006; Hafez 2006, 2007b). Christopher Reuter, meanwhile, uses the term 'suicide bombing' but is critical of the indiscriminate labelling of its perpetrators as terrorists (Reuter 2004). He favours a definition that accurately describes the nature and causes of its occurrence. Similar tendencies are discernible in the works of other scholars and commentators (Crenshaw 2007).

There is general consensus, however, that suicide bombings are a form of militant resistance and an integral part of deadly violence between state and non-state actors in the modern world. They are mainly sponsored and carried out by the weaker, non-state entities engaged in asymmetrical conflicts with well-armed state armies. They serve the political interests of the sponsoring organizations in two ways: by coercing an adversary and by giving the sponsoring organization concerned an advantage over its rival in terms of moral and material support from sympathetic constituencies or sectors of society. The evidence and analysis presented in this chapter will show that the frequency and lethality of suicide bombings have increased significantly, along with their geographical range, over the past three decades, and they are now regarded as a major threat to national and international security around the world. The data and analysis of the trends which follow are based on the Flinders University Suicide Terrorism Database.

My own initial conceptualization, or description, of suicide bombing was 'the targeted use of self-destructing humans against a perceived enemy for political ends'. However, after reviewing the studies mentioned above and other related literature, it became obvious that suicide bombing was a more complex and multidimensional phenomenon than this described. This led me to rethink its nature and scope and, in so doing, revise my conceptualization. I have attempted to capture the various dimensions of suicide bombing as follows:

Suicide bombing is lethal violence involving the targeted use of self-destructing humans against a perceived enemy to create fear and alarm in order to undermine the state's ability to maintain public order. It is associated with conflicts caused by a configuration of individual and collective actors, public and private grievances, institutional conditions and opportunity structures sanctioned by religious and political philosophies/ideologies and special group affiliations. It has significant communicative and expressive dimensions and is aimed at changing the functional principles of (mainly democratic) political systems by coercing others into actions they would not otherwise take, or into refraining from actions they desire to take. Its effectiveness is augmented by the perpetrators' willingness to die. It is a weapon of the militarily-challenged in asymmetrical conflicts and is becoming a weapon of choice among terrorist groups because of its lethality and its effectiveness in creating fear and mayhem amid the ordinary rhythm of social life.

In this book the terms 'suicide bombing', 'suicide attacks' and 'suicide terrorism' are used interchangeably. As yet, there is no comprehensive and reliable database on suicide bombings or even on terrorism. A database that claims to be relatively comprehensive is the Memorial Institute for the Prevention of Terrorism (MIPT) database, maintained by the Rand Corporation in the USA. However, this database is incomplete because of the nature of the definitions applied in the data collection. The MIPT database combines two different databases: one covering 1968 to 1997 (focusing only on international incidents, where terrorists either travelled abroad to perform their acts or selected domestic targets associated with foreign interests) and the other covering the period from 1998 to date (including both international and domestic incidents). The MIPT database aspires to completeness, yet it ignores many suicide attacks that took place in Israel and the occupied Palestinian territories, especially between 1998 and 2002. At the end of March 2008, the MIPT database was closed and its data were subsumed into the Global Terrorism Database (GTD) (2008), managed by the National Consortium for the Study of Terrorism and Responses to Terrorism (START). The GTD, while including the data contained in the MIPT's database, is structured differently and, for the intents of this study, could be viewed as more limited in its analytical power.

The Iraq Body Count (IBC) is another database that is useful but restricted in its scope. This database is confined to all incidents in Iraq since the war began in March 2003 *in which civilians have been killed.* A recent addition has been a database developed by Robert Pape of the University of Chicago using the online Lexis-Nexis data (Pape 2005). Other scholars, including Hafez (2006), Pedahzur (2005) and Gambetta (2005), have developed more specialized databases to suit their specific research purposes, although the Pedahzur database is more comprehensive than others.

The FUSTD is arguably the most comprehensive database on suicide bombings carried out globally between 1981 and 2006. The methodology to develop it involved using the existing databases – those of MIPT, Robert Pape, Mohammad Hafez, Ami Pedahzur and Diego Gambetta. The information from these databases was complemented by data and reports from the Federal Investigation Agency of Pakistan (FIA), the United States Department of State, the Institute for Peace and Conflict Studies, the South Asia Terrorism Portal, Human Rights Watch, Palestinian Human Rights Monitoring Group, Tamiltigers.net, Tamilnet, *Jerusalem Post*, the *Daily Star*, *Haaretz*, the Middle East Wire, the BBC and the *New York Times*. The analysis reported in this book relies heavily on the FUSTD.

The FUSTD has information on a range of variables. These include the date, time, country and location of attack; the name, age, gender, education, occupation, family background, nationality and marital status of the suicide bombers; the sponsoring group affiliation; a description of the conflict, weapons used, targets, and the number of fatalities and injuries. The database has gaps because information on all of the above variables was not available in many cases. At the initial stages of data collection and analysis, it became apparent that there have been many cases of suicide bombings in which more than one individual performed the attack (for example, the failed assassination attempt in 2006 on President Yusuf in Somalia in which six individual bombers were involved and that in 2003 on the then President of Pakistan, Pervez Musharraf, which involved three individuals; 9/11 is another example of a group suicide attack). These are usually referred to as 'co-ordinated attacks'.

As the FUSTD collected data both on the characteristics of individual bombers and on the attack itself (location, number of fatalities and injuries, etc.), it became important for reasons of data quality to distinguish individual attackers from individual incidents. For this reason, each individual bomber is allocated a unique identification number (individual ID), and each case of suicide bombing is allocated an incident code (incident ID). Several bombers can therefore share an incident ID but never an individual ID number. This facilitated the aggregation of the data into a new file called 'Suicide Bombing Incidents', upon which most of the analysis was performed. Where analysis was required on the characteristics of individual bombers, the 'Suicide Bombing Individual' dataset was used. As mentioned above, there are significant gaps in the data relating to individual bombers.

There are two exceptions related to the above discussion: the 7 July 2005 attacks in London and the 11 September 2001 attacks in New York and Washington, DC. These are classified as co-ordinated attacks according to the criteria applied by the sources from which data have been collected and which have been adopted in the FUSTD. However, owing to the significance of these attacks in the public mind and discourse, the composite attacks have been treated individually: four attacks for London and three for the USA. The database has records of 1,200 suicide bombing attacks carried out worldwide between 1981 and 2006. These 1,200 suicide bombing incidents involved 1,327 individuals who took part in them as suicide bombers.

Analysis

Incidence of suicide bombings and fatalities, 1981–2006

Suicide bombings were rare occurrences in the 1980s. As Figure 2.1 and the data in Table 2.1 show, by the late 1990s the number of annual

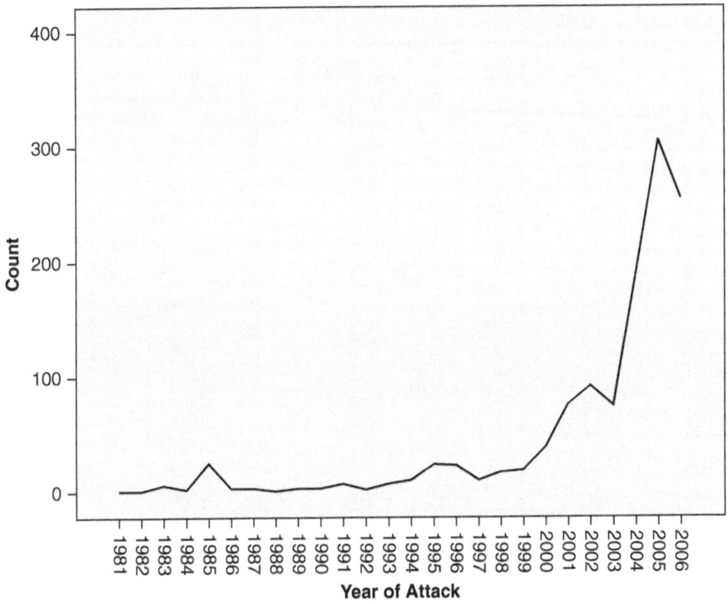

FIGURE 2.1 Suicide attacks by year, 1981–2006

TABLE 2.1 Suicide attacks worldwide, 1981–2006

Year	*Number of attacks*	*Minimum killed*	*Maximum killed*
1981	1	31	61
1982	1	62	62
1983	6	408	447
1984	2	20	29
1985	25	224	263
1986	3	9	9
1987	3	36	56
1988	1	9	9
1989	3	4	4
1990	3	9	16
1991	7	227	253
1992	2	32	38

(Continued)

TABLE 2.1 Cont'd

Year	*Number of attacks*	*Minimum killed*	*Maximum killed*
1993	7	33	35
1994	10	201	225
1995	24	317	358
1996	23	413	446
1997	10	57	160
1998	17	421	735
1999	19	56	102
2000	39	262	394
2001	76	3,324	3,420
2002	92	1,004	1,036
2003	75	795	889
2004	190	1,931	2,267
2005	306	2,572	3,026
2006	255	2,142	2,385
Total	**1,200**	**14,599**	**16,725**

Source: FUSTD 2008.
For 13 cases information on numbers killed was not available.

suicide bombing attacks had increased significantly, and for 2006 the number stood at 255. In other words there were more attacks in 2006 than there were in the twenty years between 1981 and 2000 combined. A total of 1,200 incidents of suicide bombings between 1981 and 2006 had killed between 14,600 and 16,729 people, mostly civilians. The analysis of the annual incidents shows minor peaks in 1985, 1995, 2003 and 2005–06. These peaks are related to specific conflicts, which may have elevated the incidence of suicide attacks.

The 1983–85 peak is related to the civil war in Lebanon in which a number of foreign countries were involved. The attacks were largely carried out by Hezbollah and targeted the US and French multi-national peacekeeping forces and the Israeli Defence Force (IDF) occupying southern Lebanon. These attacks led to the withdrawal of the US and French peacekeeping forces from Lebanon and forced the IDF to abandon most of the southern part of the country. The peak of the mid- to late

1990s is related to the first Palestinian intifada aimed at derailing the Oslo Peace Accord and the attacks were carried out by Hezbollah-trained members of Hamas and Palestinian Islamic Jihad (PIJ). This peak is also due to escalation of suicide bombings by Tamil Tigers in Sri Lanka. The peak in the early 2000s is related to the second or Al-Aqsa Mosque Palestinian intifada, as well as attacks by Chechen insurgents in Russia. The dramatic increase from mid-2004 to 2006 is related primarily to the Iraq War but is also due to the escalation of suicide bombing attacks in conflicts in Pakistan and Afghanistan. In summary, suicide bombings increased exponentially between 1981 and 2006 and the peaks and troughs during this period occurred as a result of the escalation of certain types of conflict.

Suicide bombings since 2006: As mentioned earlier the FUSTD is based on the analysis of suicide bombing attacks between 1981 and 2006. But suicide bombing attacks are continuing to occur, and according to the Global Terrorism Database (GTD), there were 397 suicide attacks in 2007 and 2008. These attacks occurred in twenty-two countries but 87 per cent of them were in three countries: Iraq (196), Afghanistan (80) and Pakistan (68). These attacks are not included in the following analysis because of the differences in the GTD and FUSTD methodologies. However, Appendix Table A gives the distribution of 2007–08 attacks in various countries along with resultant casualties.

Suicide bombings by country

Suicide bombings are now a global phenomenon affecting twenty-nine countries (Table 2.2). But, as we will see later, this globalization has only occurred since the late 1990s. The major sites of suicide bombings before the start of the Iraq War were Israel/Palestine, Lebanon and Sri Lanka. The other countries with a significant incidence of suicide bombings were Turkey and Chechnya/Russia. The advent of the Iraq War has seen Iraq become the most prolific site of suicide bombings; significantly, there were no incidents of suicide bombings in that country during the long and brutal regime of Saddam Hussein. Although the Iraq War began only in 2003, it accounts for a third of all deaths globally resulting from suicide bombings in the twenty-five years to 2006. In the four years between 2003 and 2006, there were twice as many suicide bombings in Iraq alone as there

TABLE 2.2 Suicide attacks by country, 1981–2006

Country	*Incidents*	*Minimum killed*	*Maximum killed*
Iraq	651	5,766	6,714
Israel/Palestinian Territories	217	1,016	1,143
Sri Lanka	93	1,172	1,647
Lebanon	48	802	912
Russia/Chechnya	28	660	798
Pakistan	49	680	708
Turkey	19	73	76
India/Kashmir	13	68	80
Afghanistan	35	198	205
Saudi Arabia	8	101	101
Indonesia	4	349	349
Egypt	4	8	8
Algeria	4	79	79
United States	3	2,988	2,988
China	2	3	3
Kuwait	2	7	14
Kenya	2	231	231
Argentina	2	115	127
United Kingdom	4	55	57
Morocco	1	47	47
Panama	1	42	42
Tanzania	1	12	251
Yemen	1	18	28
Tunisia	1	20	20
Qatar	1	1	1
Somalia	1	11	11
Jordan	1	63	63
Uzbekistan	3	12	20
Croatia	1	2	2
Total	**1,200**	**14,599**	**16,725**

Source: FUSTD 2008.
For 13 cases numbers killed were not available.

were in all other countries listed in Table 2.2 put together. While the three 9/11 attacks in New York and Washington, DC, which killed a total of 2,988 people, remain the most lethal incidents of suicide terrorism, Iraq has suffered the largest number of casualties resulting from suicide bombings in the period under review.

The lethality of suicide bombings varies as a result of three factors, namely: the hardening or protecting of targets through sound and effective counter-terrorism strategies; prompt, efficient and good medical and other emergency services; and deficient planning and execution of suicide bombings by poorly trained operatives. There is always a possibility that any suicide attack can cause horrendous numbers of casualties, as in the case of the 9/11 attacks in New York and Washington. But even there, the prompt and efficient rescue efforts of the emergency services must have saved thousands of lives.

In terms of the lethality of suicide bombings as measured by the number of people killed, Iraq topped the list by a significant margin with between five thousand and six thousand casualties, followed by Israel/Palestine and Sri Lanka with more than a thousand deaths each. But in terms of lethality per suicide attack, the 9/11 attacks were the most deadly, averaging 996 deaths per incident, followed by Kenya, Argentina and Bali/Indonesia. The attacks in Kenya targeted the US embassy and those in Argentina a Jewish synagogue. The victims of the Bali/Indonesia suicide bombings were also international, mostly Australian tourists and Indonesians.

Israel/Palestine endured the second largest number of attacks between 1981 and 2006. Since most of the attacks there are directed against Israeli Defence Force personnel and civilians, the authorities have taken steps to harden the targets chosen for suicide attacks, resulting in fewer (less than five) casualties per suicide attack. Another reason for the low number of casualties is the efficiency and effectiveness of Israel's emergency services compared with the quality of similar services in Sri Lanka and Indonesia. The low casualty rate in Afghanistan is most likely a result of the poor planning and execution of suicide bombings, but in Turkey it is most likely for the same reason as in Israel. It is probable that target hardening and poor execution of suicide bombings have kept the average casualty rate in some countries relatively low. Conversely, the relatively high average number of deaths per suicide attack in Lebanon, Chechnya/Russia, Sri Lanka, Pakistan and Saudi Arabia is possibly due to both the better execution and planning of suicide bombings and the poor quality of emergency services. This issue will be examined later in more detail.

Suicide bombings and other forms of terrorism

How destructive are suicide bombings compared with other forms of terrorism? To answer this question, data for all terrorist attacks and resulting casualties were extracted from the MIPT database and compared with the similar data for suicide bombings from the FUSTD. The data were grouped into five-yearly intervals, except for 2006 (see Table 2.3). Between 1981 and 2006, average yearly terrorist attacks multiplied almost nineteen times from 341 per year in 1981–85 to 6,653 in 2006. The corresponding increase for suicide bombings was 7 to 255 or thirty-six times. In other words, suicide terrorism has been increasing significantly faster than all other forms of terrorism in the twenty-five years between 1981 and 2006.

Most of the increases in terrorism and suicide bombings appear to have occurred since 2001. There were 9,082 terrorist attacks in the twenty years to 2000, but between 2001 and 2006 this number had increased to 20,573. Suicide bombings in the same period increased from 206 to 995,

TABLE 2.3 Deaths from suicide attacks and all forms of terrorism, 1981–2006

Year	*All terrorist attacks(n)**	*Suicide attacks(n)**	*Suicide attacks as % of all terrorist attacks*	*Deaths from all terrorist attacks(n)**	*Deaths from suicide attacks** (n)**	*Deaths from suicide attacks as % of all deaths*
1981–85	1,706	35	2	1,931	745	39
1986–90	1,755	13	1	1,926	67	4
1991–95	1,576	50	3	2,130	810	38
1996–00	4,045	108	3	4,824	1,209	25
2001–05	13,920	739	5	22,940	9,626	42
2006	6,653	255	4	12,065	2,142	18
1981–2006	29,655	1,200	4	45,816	14,599	32

Source: MIPT database and FUSTD 2008.
*n = Number.
**'Deaths from suicide attacks' refers to the minimum number killed.

a significantly higher rate of increase than the rate of non-suicide terrorism. This would suggest that suicide terrorism is becoming a weapon of choice among terrorist groups. The reason for this preference appears to be related to the destructive power of suicide bombings.

Lethality of suicide bombings

Only 4 per cent of all terrorist attacks in 1981–2006 were suicide attacks, but they accounted for 32 per cent of all terrorism-related deaths. However, these global averages do not apply universally. For example, in both Iraq and Lebanon, suicide attacks in this time period constituted 9 per cent of all terrorist attacks but with very different casualty rates: in Iraq, deaths from suicide bombings were the same as the global average at 31 per cent, but in Lebanon, the corresponding figure was more than double at 69 per cent. In Israel/Palestine, suicide bombings were 7 per cent of all terrorist attacks, resulting in 62 per cent of terrorism-related deaths (again, significantly higher than the global average). In both Chechnya/Russia and Afghanistan, suicide attacks constituted 4 per cent of all terrorist attacks but, as with Iraq and Lebanon, lead to very different death rates: in Chechnya/Russia, suicide attacks accounted for 37 per cent of terrorism-related deaths, whereas in Afghanistan, they accounted for only 13 per cent of deaths. In Pakistan, 5 per cent of all attacks were suicide attacks, accounting for 38 per cent of all terrorism-related deaths. The country-specific analysis shows the significant differences among countries most affected by suicide terrorism both in the frequency of suicide bombings and the deaths resulting from them. Iraq, Lebanon and Israel/Palestine are much more prone to suicide terrorism but have widely varying casualty rates. Compared with Israel, suicide terrorism is significantly more lethal in Iraq, Chechnya/Russia, Pakistan and Lebanon. The most likely reason for these differences lies in the relative effectiveness and efficiency of emergency services of various countries, as well as in the planning and execution of suicide attacks. Unfortunately, similar analysis is not possible for Sri Lanka because of the unavailability of the terrorism attack data required for such an analysis.

Another way to look at the comparative destructive power of suicide bombings and other forms of terrorism is to examine the average number of deaths caused by these two types. Table 2.4 shows that, globally, suicide

TABLE 2.4 Lethality of suicide attacks

Year	*Average yearly suicide attacks*	*Deaths per suicide attack**	*Average yearly non-suicide terrorist attack*	*Deaths per non-suicide terrorist attack*
1981–85	7	21	334	0.7
1986–90	3	5	348	1.1
1991–95	10	16	305	0.9
1996–00	22	11	787	0.9
2001–05	148	13	2,636	1.0
2006	255	8	6,398	1.6
1981–2006	46	12	1,094	1.1

Source: MIPT database and FUSTD 2008.
*'Deaths per suicide attack' refers to the minimum number killed.

bombings on average are twelve times more lethal than other forms of terrorism. The greater destructive power is one of the main reasons that suicide terrorism has become a method of choice among terrorist organizations. Not only is it more destructive but it is also a relatively cheap weapon to manufacture. Some estimates put the cost of preparing the suicide belt/bag and carrying out a suicide bombing attack at less than US$1,000. The most significant component is an individual volunteer, and the reports indicate that there is no shortage of volunteers in the sites of long-drawn-out military conflicts (N. Hassan 2001; Hafez 2007b; Trawick 2007). The one promising development in the data reported in Table 2.4 is that over time, the trend for the average number of deaths per suicide attack appears to be declining. This may be because the authorities in countries affected by this form of terrorism are learning how to harden the targets and making emergency services more effective and efficient in rescuing the injured after a suicide attack.

The lethality of suicide bombings also varies significantly among countries. As the data in Table 2.5 show, suicide bombings in Lebanon and Chechnya/Russia on average cause seventeen to twenty-four deaths per attack which is significantly higher than the global average of twelve. In Iraq, the corresponding figure is nine. But in Israel and Afghanistan, the casualty figures are the lowest at five and six respectively. Again, these outcomes are due to different reasons. In Israel, the effective counter-terrorism measures and

TABLE 2.5 Suicide bombings and deaths arising from them as a proportion of all terrorism in selected countries, 1981–2006

*Country*****	*As % of all terrorist attacks**	*Suicide bombings/ all terrorist attacks*	*As % of all terrorism deaths***	*Suicide bombing deaths/all terrorism deaths*	*Deaths per suicide bombing*	*Ratio****
Iraq	9	651/7,400	31	5,767/18,865	9	1: 4.5
Israel/ Palestine	7	217/3,167	61	1,016/1,664	5	1: 22.3
Lebanon	9	48/540	69	802/1,162	17	1: 22.9
Chechnya/ Russia	4	28/792	37	660/1,791	24	1: 14.4
Pakistan	5	49/952	38	680/1,784	14	1: 11.4
Afghanistan	4	35/962	13	198/1,582	6	1: 4.1

Source: MIPT database and FUSTD 2008.
*Suicide bombing as a percentage of all terrorist attacks.
**Deaths from suicide bombing as percentage of all terrorism related deaths.
***Ratio of average deaths from non-suicide bombing terrorism to average deaths from suicide bombing.
****Sri Lanka was omitted because the lack of data on 'all terrorist' attacks.

the efficiency of the state's emergency services probably explain the low casualty rates, but in the case of Afghanistan, the reasons are likely to be poor planning and execution of attacks.

What is really striking is that, notwithstanding all its counter-terrorism policies and efficient emergency services, Israel still suffers the highest rate of deaths from suicide terrorism attacks. The same applies to Lebanon. Iraq and Afghanistan, on the other hand, have only a third of the global average of twelve deaths per suicide attack, and that, as noted earlier, is most likely a result of poor planning and execution of such attacks. These figures provide some insights into why the Israeli government and society are so sensitive to suicide attacks and take very strong punitive actions against the perpetrators. In the cases of Israel and Lebanon, suicide attacks pose a significantly greater threat to the social fabric of society and polity. But again, the Israeli government's policies towards the Palestinians and the Sri Lankan and Russian governments' policies towards Tamil and Chechen populations respectively have tended to produce equally violent and ruthless responses.

TABLE 2.6 Targets of suicide bombings by selected countries, 1981–2006 (%)

Targets	*Global*	*Iraq*	*Israel/ Palestine*	*Sri Lanka*	*Lebanon*	*Pakistan*	*Chechnya/ Russia*	*Afghanistan*
Infrastructure	11	13	5	12	6	–	31	3
Local Security/ Public officials	45	50	29	69	42	44	35	38
Foreign forces/ contractors	9	11	1	–	46	9	4	12
Civilians	30	21	63	12	6	24	31	24
Others	5	4	2	8	0	24	0	24
Total	**100**	**100**	**100**	**101***	**100**	**101***	**101***	**101***

Source: FUSTD 2008.
*Percentages rounded up.

Targets and types of suicide bombings

Tables 2.6 and 2.7 contain analysis of data pertaining to targets and the weapons used in executing suicide bombings, both globally and in the six main sites: Iraq, Israel/Palestine, Sri Lanka, Lebanon, Pakistan and Afghanistan. The FUSTD data pertaining to the targets were classified into broad categories: infrastructure (pipelines, buildings, merchant vessels, oil tankers, radio stations, official buildings); local security and public officials (police, checkpoints, local military patrols and vehicles, government officials

TABLE 2.7 Types of suicide bombing by selected countries (%)

Weapon	*Global*	*Iraq*	*Israel/ Palestine*	*Sri Lanka*	*Lebanon*	*Pakistan*	*Chechnya/ Russia*	*Afghanistan*
SVA	56	72	19	43	90	20	39	37
SBA	40	28	66	46	10	77	61	57
Others*	4	0.4	15	11	0	3	0	7
Total	**100**	**101****	**100**	**100**	**100**	**100**	**100**	**101****

Source: FUSTD 2008.
SVA = Suicide Vehicular Attack.
SBA = Suicide Belt/Bag Attack.
*Others include conflicting reports.
**Percentages rounded up.

and ministers); foreign military forces/contractors (military personnel, vehicles, bases, embassies, foreign private security companies and personnel, foreign private contractors); civilians (individuals, shops and restaurants, civilian vehicles, public transport, etc.); and others (multiple/indistinguishable targets, UN, Red Cross, religious sites).

The data about the weapons used (i.e. the type of suicide bombing) were classified into four broad categories, namely: vehicle-borne improvised explosive device (VBIED, or car and truck bomb); improvised explosive device (IED, or suicide belt/bag) carried by the suicide bomber; other (suicide shooting attack); and conflicting (where data sources differ as to the weapon used). The data for targets and weapons used for many incidents of suicide bombings were not available. Tables 2.6 and 2.7, therefore, report only the suicide bombing incidents for which the data on the target of the attacks and weapons used were available.

Globally, the local security forces were the target of 45 per cent of suicide bombing incidents and, if foreign security forces and contractors are included, then 54 per cent of attacks were launched against them. The other two main targets were infrastructure (11 per cent) and civilians (30 per cent). As for the weapons used, vehicle-borne improvised explosive devices were the most common globally, followed by improvised explosive devices. In 4 per cent of cases, other types of weapons such as firearms and grenades were used. One inference that can be drawn from the data pertaining to targets is that weaker groups involved in asymmetrical endemic conflicts use suicide bombings as a weapon of war. The stronger groups in the conflict do not resort to these weapons.

How do countries that are the main sites of suicide bombings differ from the global pattern? Iraq, the primary site of such attacks in the world now, follows the global pattern closely, suggesting that insurgents in Iraq are actively seeking to destabilize the country by targeting its security forces, public officials, infrastructure and the coalition supporters of the new government. As Cordesman (2005) and Hafez (2007b) have pointed out, the main aims of the Iraqi insurgents are to drive out the US and coalition forces, overthrow the new Iraqi government and deprive it of popular legitimacy, keep Iraqi forces from becoming effective and create a climate of general insecurity in the country. The choice of targets for the insurgent attacks would support this strategy of destabilization. Iraqi civilians are the most likely targets because of the sectarian nature of the evolving war in the country in which Iraqi Sunnis, Shias and Kurds are targeting each other to avenge past and present injustices, grievances and religious antipathies.

The analysis of the Israeli and Palestinian conflict follows a strikingly different pattern. The Palestinian suicide bombers fighting for the political destiny of their homeland are no match for the overwhelming superiority of the Israeli Defence Force. Additionally, over the years of its drawn-out and violent military conflict with the Palestinians, Israel has developed effective strategies to protect its soldiers. Palestinian fighters see civilians as legitimate targets, as indeed does the Israeli state when it punishes the families and communities of suicide bombers. It is almost impossible for any government to protect its civilian populations from terrorist attacks all the time, thus rendering them a soft target for suicide bombings. Given this type of configuration, it is not surprising to find that Israeli civilians are the most frequent targets of Palestinian suicide bombings.

The Sri Lankan situation is almost the mirror image of the Israeli situation with local security and public officials being the main targets of Tamil Tiger suicide bombings. The conflict in which the Tamil Tigers were fighting for a separate homeland for Sri Lankan Tamils is typical of a formal war between two adversaries. The data for Lebanon, Pakistan and Afghanistan are comparatively less robust than those from Iraq, Israel/Palestine and Sri Lanka. The distribution of targets in Lebanon has some affinity with the Israel/Palestine situation. In the case of Lebanon, foreign forces were the main targets. This reflects the situation in that country where for twenty years the Israeli Defence Force (IDF) occupied a large part of the south, thus making the IDF not only a convenient but also a strategic target of suicide bombing missions sponsored by Hezbollah and other insurgent groups. The distributions of targets in Pakistan and Afghanistan are similar to the global patterns as well as to Iraqi patterns. The use of suicide bombings in the conflicts in Pakistan and Afghanistan is comparatively new and is likely to change as fighting between adversaries evolves further.

In terms of the weapons employed in committing suicide bombing attacks, the two main types are VBIED and IED. The other forms of weapons used refer mainly to suicide shooting attacks. In a significant number of suicide bombings, it was not possible to determine the type of weapon used in the attack from the available information. Globally, 56 per cent of suicide bombings used VBIEDs, and in 40 per cent of incidents IEDs were used. The analysis of data shows significant differences between countries. In Iraq, 72 per cent of suicide attacks were carried out by VBIEDs and 28 per cent by IEDs. It is not clear why, but in Iraq the use of the two main weapons differs according to the intended target. According to one study, 70 per cent of all coalition casualties are caused by IEDs but 60 per cent of all Iraqi casualties are caused by VBIEDs. According to some estimates, 50 per cent of all VBIEDs in Iraq were suicide attacks (Cordesman 2005).

In Israel/Palestine, the distribution of weapons used was almost the opposite of that in Iraq, with the most common method appearing to be the IED. Unfortunately, there are big gaps in the data pertaining to the weapons used, and it is difficult to say this conclusively. However, given the security and surveillance exercised by the Israeli army in the Palestinian territories, it is not surprising that this kind of weapon is the most frequent method used by the perpetrators: it is relatively inexpensive and logistically easier to manufacture and use. These two conditions would make the IED the preferred weapon in the context of Israel/Palestine. In Sri Lanka, the attacks for which data are available reveal that both VBIEDs and IEDs are more or less equally used. Tamil Sea Tigers use boats to carry out suicide attacks against the Sri Lankan navy, but on land they mostly use both methods.

In Lebanon, the attacks were overwhelmingly carried out using VBIEDs, but in Pakistan it was the opposite. The data for both Lebanon and Pakistan are relatively incomplete, and therefore at best only tentative conclusions can be drawn at present about weapons used. In the case of Afghanistan, the data are a little more robust, and they show that IEDs are the most common weapon used in suicide attacks. The usefulness of the data about weapons is that they can be applied in order to develop appropriate strategies for the prevention of such attacks by disrupting the supply chain and manufacture of such weapons.

Concluding remarks

Suicide bombing is the fastest-growing form of terrorism, now affecting at least twenty-nine countries worldwide. In the twenty-five years to 2006, suicide bombings have increased by fifty times whereas incidents of terrorism have increased by nineteen times. The FUSTD is the most comprehensive database available to analyse this growth and its consequences. The analysis reported in this chapter shows that 1,200 incidents of suicide bombings between 1981 and 2006 caused between 14,600 and 16,729 deaths and injured as many as ten times more people. While constituting only 4 per cent of all terrorist attacks in the period covered by this study, suicide bombings accounted for 32 per cent of all terrorism-related deaths, making this type of attack on average twelve times more lethal than other forms of terrorism. It is this destructive power that has made suicide bombing the weapon of choice among the terrorist groups.

The other reasons for the increasing popularity of suicide bombing among the terrorist groups include its major psychological impact and high media coverage; its symbolic significance and appeal as an act of exceptional dedication, commitment, martyrdom and sacrifice for one's political community; its importance for the political and financial mobilization of the sponsoring groups in the community; and finally, its effectiveness in attracting potential suicide bombers. The observed variations in the lethality of suicide bombings can be attributed to the level of sophistication of each country's counter-terrorism measures, the emergency response services, including the medical emergency service, fire brigade and the police, as well as the quality of planning, training and delivery of the suicide attacks. The Iraq War has undoubtedly given a boost to suicide terrorism and it appears to be spreading rapidly to other countries in the region, particularly Pakistan and Afghanistan.

The main targets of suicide bombings, except in Israel, are the security forces and public officials, suggesting that it is a weapon of war used by the non-state actors in an endemic and violent conflict. In Israel, civilians are the main target of Palestinian suicide bombings. I have argued that Palestinian groups fighting Israel are militarily weak and unable to attack the well-equipped and highly-trained Israeli army, and thus they attack softer targets. The Palestinian groups also see civilians as an integral part of the conflict arising from Israel's occupation of Palestinian territories.

Globally, VBIEDs (or car and truck bombs) are the main weapon used by suicide terrorists. This is largely a result of the high numbers of suicide bombings taking place in Iraq. In Israel/Palestine, Sri Lanka, Pakistan and Afghanistan, IEDs (or suicide belts/bags) are the most commonly used weapon. Unfortunately, the data pertaining to the targets and weapons are not sufficiently robust to conduct a more thorough and grounded analysis. This information could be useful in developing appropriate strategies to counter suicide terrorism by destroying or disrupting the supply chain of material for the production of these weapons.

3
EXPLAINING SUICIDE BOMBINGS

Explanations of suicide bombings can be grouped into three broad categories. The first category would include explanations that frame causes of suicide bombing in terms of the personal characteristics and motivations of the individual perpetrator. The second category includes explanations that conceptualize suicide bombing attacks as instrumental and strategic weapons used by sponsoring organizations that represent the weaker party in asymmetrical conflicts. They are seen as benefiting the political organizations that use them in two ways: by coercing an adversary, and by giving an organization an advantage over its rival in terms of support from constituencies. The third category includes explanations that overlap with the above two but self-consciously focus on societal conditions. These conditions may include the oppressive occupation of the 'homeland' by a powerful enemy. The occupation is characterized by policies and practices that seek to devalue the cultural codes of honour and shame of the subject group, creating widely felt experiences of humiliation. Such societal conditions are conducive to the rise of altruistic sacrifice for the honourable survival of one's community; they also encourage the growth of social movements that are non-institutionalized, spontaneous social alliances of people protesting about widespread grievances. These three explanatory frameworks, along with some of the studies that fall in the purview of each, will be discussed in this chapter.

Explanations focusing on individual characteristics and motivations

Explanations of suicide bombings focusing on the characteristics and motivations of individual perpetrators cover factors ranging from socio-economic characteristics, such as poverty and lack of education, to psychopathology. They view suicide bombings as a pathological phenomenon carried out by individuals suffering from serious social and psychological impairments. The confluence of two widely held Western perceptions of suicide and terrorism appears to be an important cause underpinning such explanations. Suicide is commonly viewed as psychopathological behaviour and not as an outcome of rational calculations by the victim. This view is related to the increasing medicalization of suicide as an illness. Suicide has come to be seen first and foremost as pathological and psychologically deviant behaviour and is treated and studied on those terms. (For a general discussion see Silke 2007a; R. Hassan 1995; Grimland, Apter and Kerkhof 2006; Townsend 2007; Lester, Yang and Lindsay 2004).

In much the same way, the study of terrorism has been dominated by the widely held perception that terrorists are mad and bad men and women. Many psychological theories postulate that terrorists suffer from various forms of mental deficiency and personality disorder. Terrorists are widely portrayed as psychopaths, paranoids, homicidal criminals and narcissistic. These stereotypes continue to dominate contemporary debates and find, in the imagination and expectations of the general public, a receptive and satisfied audience. The combination of two apparently pathological phenomena has heavily biased the contemporary consideration of suicide bombers as sick, crazy, criminal, homicidal killers and deranged fanatics, dismissing the possibility that suicides and terrorists might be rational, reasonable and ordinary individuals. Consequently, the causes of the problem are attributed to pathological predispositions of individual perpetrators and not to society as a whole. Suicide terrorists are labelled as crazed cowards bent on senseless destruction. Societal responses to the phenomenon consequently have focused on restraining, incarcerating, proscribing and, if need be, killing the offending individuals (Silke 2003, 2007a; Atran 2003; Berko 2007; Gilligan 2000; R. Hassan 2001; Gupta and Mundra 2005; Israeli 2003; Reuter 2004; Rapoport 2002).

The modern era of suicide bombings began in the 1980s in Lebanon, where bombings were carried out by Shia Muslim organizations, Hezbollah and Amal, and by secular nationalist parties, the Syrian Nationalist Party, Lebanese Communist Party and Lebanese Baath Party. The tactic then spread to the Liberation Tigers of Tamil Eelam (LTTE), who spearheaded the Tamil insurgency against the Sri Lankan government, and was then adopted by the Palestinian groups Hamas and Palestinian Islamic Jihad (PIJ), who were fighting the Israeli occupation of the Palestinian territories. The predominantly Middle Eastern origin of suicide bombing has played a significant role in the formulation of the individualistic and pathological explanations offered in some of the early studies of the phenomenon. This may have been influenced by stereotypes of Arabs/Muslims in the Israeli media and society as being irrational, violent, dangerous, manipulative, helpless, inefficient and passive (Orbach 2004; Barzilai 2001). Much of the early psychological research on terrorism instructed that the main causes of terrorism 'must be sought in the psychopathology of the assassin' (Kaplan 1981: 36).

Others found the genesis of the phenomenon in psychopathic and paranoid personality disorders (Post 1986; Pearlstein 1991; deMause 2002). Such views have had a powerful impact on government policy decisions around the world. Personal risk factors feature prominently in studies by clinical theoreticians (Kobrin 2002), which, on the basis of analysing the backgrounds and documents left by the 9/11 attackers, report that Mohammad Atta's father was a stubborn control freak and Atta was possessively close to his mother until college. Such personal background factors, together with Atta's prohibition of women touching his dead body or attending his funeral, led Kobrin to conclude that a regressed emotional state contributed to his motivation for carrying out the 9/11 attacks as they fulfilled a latent wish to fuse with the pre-Oedipal mother through death. Symbolically, the USA (and Israel) is the bad mother who rejects the child (the Palestinian/Muslim) who is yearning for her. The USA (and Israel) is the maternal object whom the suicide attacker wishes not only to destroy but also to fuse with in a wedding of blood. Kobrin claims that the dynamic of yearning for fusion with a loved and hated mother could be clearly identified in some of the 9/11 attackers. While Kobrin emphasises the dynamics of fusion with a rejecting but loved mother, Stein (2002) focuses on the wish to fuse with a powerful and feared father. To Stein, the suicide attack is a blood wedding with the ultimate paternal figure who demands the ultimate sacrifice.

Popular images of crazed terrorists embarking on a killing spree through suicide terrorism encouraged public support for this approach (Atran 2003: 5). Sections of the popular Israeli press continue to push the idea that Palestinian suicide bombers take drugs or alcohol before they are sent on their suicide missions. As in the case of the Assassins of twelfth-century Iran mentioned in Chapter 1, such stories are incorrect. Extensive tests on the remains of suicide bombers by Israel's Institute of Forensic Medicine has led the Institute's authorities to declare that suicide terrorists were free from the influence of drugs and were fully lucid at the time of their death, and that their actions were driven by psychological motives prior to the suicide attack itself (Goldenberg 2002).

According to the Israeli psychologist Ariel Merari, 'Culture in general, and religion in particular seem to be relatively unimportant in the phenomenon of terrorist suicide. Terrorist suicide, like any other suicide, is basically an individual rather than a group phenomenon: it is done by people who wish to die for personal reasons' (Merari 1990: 206). Merari's view is echoed in the studies of R. Israeli, another leading Israeli academic at the Hebrew University's Truman Institute for Peace, who maintains that suicide bombers are individuals with low self-esteem who have emerged from broken families (Israeli 1997). Yet other commentators have suggested that the motivation of Islamist suicide bombers 'is firmly embedded in collective psyche' (Gunaratna 2002: 10).

The tendency for people to explain and interpret behaviour exclusively in terms of individual personality and personal factors is found to be especially prevalent in the 'individualistic' cultures of the West (Atran 2003: 1535–36). In the case of suicide bombing, it arises from the prevalent proclivity of intellectual workers (including journalists, scholars and researchers) to explain suicide terrorism by assembling the life narratives of individual and often specific suicide bombers.

> These life narratives follow a familiar pattern. Typically, the writer begins by interviewing the suicide bomber's immediate family, friends, and other close associates, asking detailed questions about the personal history and psychological conditions of the individual. From these interviews, the suicide attacker's life history is stitched together, often with painstaking effort to identify the key moments of transition that 'caused' the person to wish to die and so to

> willingly accept a suicide terrorist mission. Finally, there is a summary of the statement – often to the effect that, much to the writer's surprise, no clear 'moment of transition' could be found.
>
> *(Pape 2005: 171)*

This method is called psychological autopsy and is used by psychiatrists and psychologists to explain causes of ordinary suicides. But there is a conceptual gap that confounds efforts to explain what motivates individual suicide bombers because of the underlying assumption of this approach that all suicides arise from similar causes (Davis 2003; Victor 2003; Berko 2007; Schweitzer 2007). In modern psychiatry, suicide is regarded as an end, an exit from unbearable existential conditions, accompanied by acute emotional pain, that drives people to take their own lives. Our personal experiences and the contents of media reports that highlight the personal trauma or mental illness of the suicide victim, reinforce this common understanding. Such understanding of ordinary suicide leads to common misunderstanding about suicide bombers: that they are seeking to end their lives to escape from a personal emotional pain in a dramatic manner. This is called a 'fundamental attribution error', a tendency to explain behaviour in terms of individual traits, even when significant situational factors in society at large are at work (Atran 2003: 1536; Pape 2005: 172; Silke 2007a).

Attempts to develop psychological profiles of suicide bombers have not produced many fruitful results. Macro-level studies that have examined a commonly held stereotype, popular with politicians and even some scholars, that the root cause of terrorism is poverty and economic deprivation have found no connection between poverty and terrorism. In fact, the results point in the opposite direction: a higher living standard is positively associated with support for or participation in terrorism (Maleckova 2005; Krueger and Maleckova 2003). Micro-level studies have failed to find a stable set of demographic, socioeconomic, religious and psychological variables that can be causally linked to terrorist personality. In fact, such studies have often produced contradictory results (Victoroff 2005). Still, this line of inquiry remains attractive around the world, especially in psychologically oriented studies. Labels like mad and bad, fanatics, homicidal killers or insane may or may not serve a useful function for legal purposes. But if the purpose is to learn and understand the causes and prevention of suicide terrorism, then the labels simply enable us to close our minds and diminish our desire to understand its real nature and purpose (Gilligan 2000; Horgan 2003; Silke 2007a; Victoroff 2005).

Studies and literature on Islamic radicalization show that there was no clear link between individual factors, including age, gender, education, career, marital status and religion, and becoming a terrorist. In relation to Islam, evidence shows that 'individuals were not becoming radicalized because of the efforts of an Al Qaeda recruiter, but rather the process was occurring independently of the established jihadis' (Silke 2007a: 111). Societal processes such as social marginalization appeared to be a common factor in the backgrounds of most jihadi recruits in the West, but that did not mean that *all* or even most marginalized people were members of terrorist groups.

So, are suicide bombers mindless fanatics or mindful martyrs? Why do they adopt this fatalistic role? According to the results of a recent study of over four hundred members of Al Qaeda, three quarters of them came from the upper or middle classes. This study by psychiatrist Marc Sageman also found other evidence of the normality and even superiority of these youths turned suicide bombers. The majority, 90 per cent, came from caring, intact families. Two thirds had gone to college; two thirds were married; and most had children and jobs in science and engineering. According to Sageman, they are the best and brightest of their society in many ways (Sageman 2004; see also Shermer 2006: 33).

One consistent finding of studies exploring pathways to terrorism is that involvement in terrorism is a gradual process – typically occurring over a period of years. Most terrorists become radicalized as members of a small group of like-minded individuals. The relative isolation of the individuals from the surrounding society beforehand appears to play an important role in creating group cohesion, solidarity and sense of common purpose. Existing social science evidence makes it clear that terrorists cannot simply be regarded as typical members of society: on the contrary, they are a distinct group, and in many ways the origins of their unconventional behaviour are exceptional. From a psychological standpoint, with the exception of a few rare cases, there is no apparent connection between violent militant activity and personality disorders (Ricolfi 2005; Silke 2003, 2007a; Sageman 2004; Hopgood 2005).

Becoming a terrorist involves a highly selective process, which explains why most terrorist groups have only a few pathological members. Indeed, candidates who exhibit signs of psychopathology or other mental illness are rejected in the interests of group survival. Terrorist groups need members whose behaviour appears to be normal and who would not arouse suspicion. A member who exhibits traits of psychopathy or any noticeable degree of mental illness would only be a liability for the group, whatever his or her skills. That individual could not be depended on to carry out the assigned mission. On the contrary, such an individual would be more likely to sabotage the group by, for example, botching an operation or revealing group secrets if captured. Nor would a psychotic member be likely to enhance group solidarity. This type of screening has been reported for a number of groups who sponsor suicide terror attacks in the modern world (Hudson 1999; Ricolfi 2005; Silke 2007a; Pape 2005; Argo 2004).

Suicide bombing as organizational imperative and strategic weapon

A number of studies explicitly or implicitly argue that non-state sponsoring organizations use suicide bombing attacks as an instrumental and strategic weapon in their conflicts with well-equipped state armies. Invariably, the sponsoring organizations represent the weaker party in these asymmetrical conflicts, and this applies even to regular armies, like the Japanese army in World War II, when they resorted to using suicide missions as a tactical weapon. In almost all cases, it is a weapon of last resort and a minuscule part of the sponsoring organization's arsenal of weapons. For example, Hezbollah, Hamas, Al-Aqsa Martyrs Brigades, Liberation Tigers of Tamil Eelan, Taliban, Al Qaeda, Al Qaeda in Iraq (AQI) and the Kurdistan Workers Party all have used other options.

Suicide bombings are not the exclusive domain of militant Islamic organizations either: they are used by organizations with diverse religious and ideological affiliations. Suicide bombers are not clad with clerical robes, but don flags, uniforms and revolutionary beards too. Between 1981 and 2003, only 34.6 per cent of suicide bombing missions were carried out by Islamic groups; 52.8 per cent were carried out by secular groups, while the remainder were carried out by groups of unknown ideological and religious affiliations (Gambetta 2005: 261–62). As Figure 3.1 shows, as far as targets are concerned, suicide bombings target enemy soldiers and equipment as well as political and symbolic objectives.

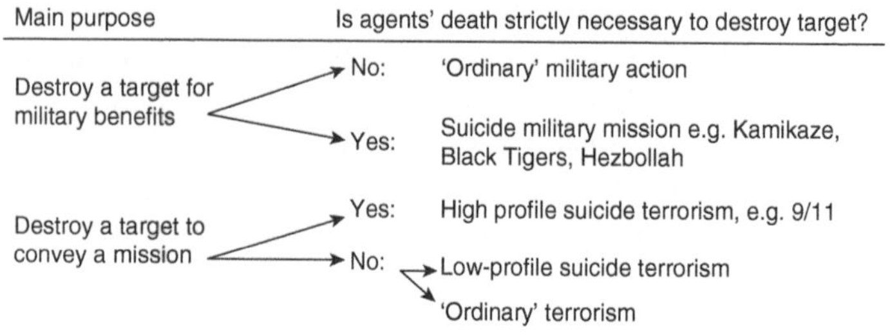

FIGURE 3.1 Types of suicide mission by organizational goals and relevance of agents' death

Source: Gambetta (2005: 264).

Commenting on the rationality of terrorist organizations, Martha Crenshaw has pointed out that efficacy is the primary standard used by terrorist organizations to achieve their political goals. As mentioned earlier, suicide terror is rarely, if ever, the strategy of first choice, tending rather to follow other strategies deemed less effective through the process of trial and error. 'Organizations arrive at collective judgements about the relative effectiveness of different strategies ... on the basis of observation and experience, as much as on the basis of abstract strategic conceptions derived from ideological assumptions – allowing for social learning' (Crenshaw 1990: 8).

Suicide bombings are mechanically simple, versatile and tactically efficient for reaching well-guarded, high-value targets. Compared with non-suicide terrorist attacks, they are significantly more lethal in terms of the casualties they inflict on the enemy (see Chapter 2). Moreover, they are effective in terrifying the enemy and have high symbolic value in signalling resolve and dedication to the cause. They are also difficult to deter because of the perpetrator's willingness to die. Researchers subscribing to this perspective believe that understanding the organization's rationale is more important in explaining suicide attacks than understanding individuals' motivations (Gambetta 2005; Pape 2005; Bloom 2005; Gupta and Mundra 2005; Hoffman and McCormick 2004).

For the sponsoring organizations, suicide attacks serve multiple purposes. They mobilize sympathetic supporters and attract recruits and financial support. The death of the perpetrator is used to legitimize his or her action. These influences are reciprocal: organizations use suicide bombing attacks to generate support, but at the same time they respond to popular demand. The ultimate goals are political and not religious. Religion can mobilize both support and participation because of its emphasis on redemption and martyrdom, but is not required. When present, it is often combined with nationalism and ethnic and community solidarity. The suicide attacks are driven by a cocktail of emotions including pride, anger, rage, humiliation, shame, hopelessness and honour. They convey the message that we may be materially weak but we are powerful because we do not fear death (Crenshaw 2007; Pape 2005; Khosrokhavar 2005; Gambetta 2005; Bloom 2005; Oliver and Steinberg 2005; Reuter 2004; Hoffman and McCormick 2004; Berman and Laitin 2005).

The work of two US political scientists, Robert Pape and Mia Bloom, best exemplifies the strategic logic approach to explaining suicide attacks and is discussed here in some detail. In their respective contributions, they show that suicide attacks pay off for the sponsoring organization in two possible ways: by coercing an adversary and by giving it an advantage over its rival in terms of support from constituencies or sectors of society. According to Robert Pape, modern suicide terrorism is mainly a response to foreign occupation of the homeland. He makes a strong claim that campaigns of suicide terrorism are carried out by organized groups for a specific political goal – to end this foreign occupation. So the core phenomenon to be explained is not an individual suicide attack but the existence of protracted suicide terrorist campaigns. The strategic logic of suicide terrorism is aimed at political coercion.

> The vast majority of suicide attacks are not isolated or random acts by individual fanatics but rather occur in clusters as part of larger campaigns by an organise group to achieve a specific goal. Moreover, the main goals of suicide terrorist groups are profoundly this-worldly. Suicide terrorist campaigns are primarily nationalistic, not religious, nor are they particularly Islamic ... every group mounting a suicide campaign over the past two decades has had as a major objective – or as its central objective – coercing a foreign state that has military forces in what the terrorists see as their homeland to take those forces out. Further, all of the target states have been democracies, which terrorists see as more vulnerable to coercion than other types of regime.
> *(Pape 2005: 21)*

Suicide attacks magnify the coercive effects of punishment because they are more destructive than other types of terrorism and they effectively signal future attacks. The evidence tends to support Pape. Hezbollah-sponsored suicide attacks compelled the US and French military forces to abandon Lebanon in 1983 and Israeli forces to leave that country in 1985 and the Gaza Strip and West Bank in 1994 and 1995. Similarly, in the late 1990s Tamil Tigers' suicide attacks in Sri Lanka and PKK attacks in Turkey won LTTE and the Kurds significant concessions from the Sri Lankan and Turkish governments respectively. This displays what Pape calls the coercive logic of suicide terrorism and has led to its rapid increase because terrorists have learned that this strategy pays, i.e. is effective.

Two other characteristics of organizations sponsoring suicide terrorism increase their effectiveness. Unlike primarily criminal organizations or religious cults, suicide terrorism groups command broad social support within the national communities from which they recruit, because they are seen as pursuing legitimate nationalist goals, especially liberation of the homeland from foreign occupation. This also enhances social integration and creates a climate of altruism in their community that can lead normal individuals to volunteer for suicide missions out of a sense of duty. Few suicide bombers are social misfits, criminally insane or professional losers. Typically, they are psychologically normal, have better than average economic prospects, are deeply integrated into social networks and are emotionally attached to their national communities. They see themselves as sacrificing their lives for the nation's good. Figure 3.2 describes the causal logic of Pape's model of suicide terrorism. For Pape:

> The bottom line, then, is that suicide terrorism is mainly a response to foreign occupation. Isolated incidents in other circumstances do occur. Religion plays a role. However, modern suicide terrorism is

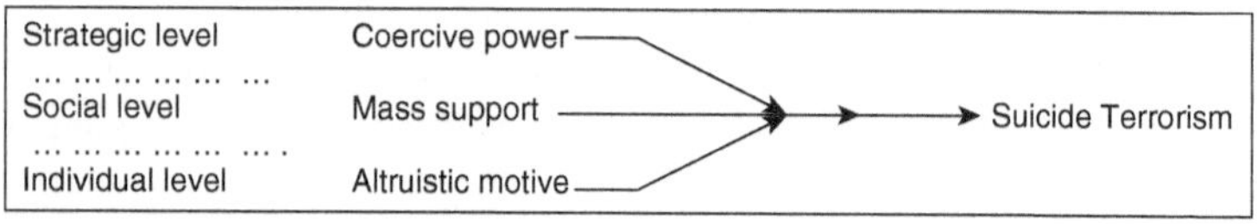

FIGURE 3.2 Causal logic of suicide terrorism

Source: Pape 2005: 22.

> best understood as an extreme strategy for national liberation against democracies with troops that pose an imminent threat to control the territory the terrorists view as their homeland.
>
> *(Pape 2005: 23)*

Pape's model has received a number of criticisms. Martha Crenshaw has criticized it for arbitrarily excluding isolated attacks so that such incidents that 'would be inconvenient to explain are thus omitted' (Crenshaw 2007: 142). She is also critical of Pape for lumping different groups together in a common campaign, such as Iraqi rebels, and not distinguishing between Al Qaeda and local affiliates or start-ups. She also questions whether suicide terror campaigns actually pay. Pape marshals evidence showing that six of thirteen completed campaigns between 1983 and 2001 resulted in 'no change' in the foreign occupation and five other campaigns were continuing (Pape 2005: 40). For Pape, a 50 per cent success rate would be remarkable, since in general coercion works in international politics only one-third of the time. In particular, the success rate of campaigns may be not as realistic as he claims. His conclusion that Sri Lanka would grant Tamil autonomy in 2001 was premature, especially in view of the routing of LTTE by the Sri Lankan army in early 2009. Others have also criticised Pape along similar lines (Moghadam 2006, 2008; Brym and Araj 2006, 2008; Roberts 2007).

The FUSTD, for major campaigns between 1981 and 2006, also provides only partial validation of Pape's hypothesis (see Table 3.1) and supports Crenshaw's observation that even if we accept (a) the idea of a campaign as the unit of analysis, (b) the coding of the outcomes of the completed campaigns and (c) the cost-benefit ratios as something under 50, Pape's conclusion at best receives only qualified support. But perhaps the most serious problem not dealt with by Pape is that suicide bombings have high costs (arrests, assassinations of leaders, collateral damage, destruction of houses, road blocks and checkpoints), which are not offset by any concessions that the government might give and have lasting psychological, social and economic costs.

More recently, Hafez's study of suicide bombers in Iraq has also raised issues about the universal applicability of Pape's theory (Hafez 2007b). Hafez agrees that the strategic logic of suicide attacks appears to conform to the facts in Iraq. Suicide terrorism did not exist in Iraq before the US-led invasion.

TABLE 3.1 Selected suicide terrorism campaigns, 1981–2006

Region	*Dispute*	*Terrorist group*	*Terrorist goal*	*No attacks*	*No killed*	*Democracy a target*	*Outcome*
Lebanon 1981–2006	US/F/IDF military presence	Hezbollah	US/F/IDF withdrawal	48	802	Yes	Complete withdrawal
Israel/Gaza West Bank 1993–2006	IDF military presence Various disputes	Hamas PIJ Al-Aqsa	IDF withdrawal/ National Liberation	217	1016	Yes	IDF Withdrawal from Gaza/TBD
Afghanistan 2001–06	NATO/US military presence	Taliban	NATO/US withdrawal	35	198	Yes	TBD
Sri Lanka 1987–2006	SL military presence	LTTE Tamil Tigers	SL withdrawal	93	1172	Yes	Negotiations/TBD*
Turkey 1996–2006	Turkey military presence	PKK	Turkey withdrawal	19	73	Yes	Partial success cultural/political concessions
Iraq 2003–06	US military presence	Insurgent groups	US withdrawal	651	5766	Yes	TBD
Chechnya 2000–06	Russia military presence	Chechnya Rebels	Russian withdrawal	28	660	Yes	TBD
India/Kashmir 2000–06	Indian military presence	Kashmir Rebels	Indian withdrawal	13	68	Yes	TBD
Saudi Arab/US 1996–06	US military presence	Al Qaeda	US withdrawal	11	3089	No	TBD

Source: FUSTD 2008.

*The LTTE was defeated by the Sri Lankan Army in 2009 but the Tamil-Sinhalese conflict remains unresolved.

TBD = To be determined.

The link between suicide attacks and occupation of 'homeland' is therefore apparent but is far from being a causal one. First, while the majority of Iraqi insurgents are Iraqis, a large percentage of suicide bombers are not. Furthermore, most suicide attacks in Iraq are directed not at the foreign forces but at the Iraqi security forces and civilians. One can explain their presence and actions by accepting that their worldview rejects nationalistic borders and deems Muslim unity as the sole legitimate basis for their identification and jihad, which means 'religion matters' (Hafez 2007b: 215).

This also raises the question of the nature of suicide terrorists' altruism since they are not integrated into the reality of Iraqi society. Most Iraqis are Shia Arab and Kurd, whereas most suicide bombers are Sunni militants. In Pape's defence, one can argue that the altruism of suicide bombers in Iraq is derived not from local but from global Islam (Roy 2004; Khosrokhavar 2005). Their attacks are means to achieving multiple goals, which may include expulsion of foreign occupying forces from an Islamic land, establishing an Islamic state in Iraq, and sacrificing their lives for the realization of these goals as a project of their identity grounded in a globalized Islam.

Gaining a competitive edge

In her book *Dying to Kill*, the US political scientist Mia Bloom offers the competitive outbidding hypothesis of suicide terrorism, which also focuses on the organizations sponsoring suicide terrorism and not on the individual perpetrator's proclivities and personal traits. Bloom agrees that the key objective of suicide terrorism is to end foreign occupation of the homeland and secure its autonomy and independence. She postulates that the main attraction of suicide terrorism for the sponsoring organization is that it enhances its prestige and gives it an advantage in intra-movement competition for recruits, money and publicity. Effectiveness, then, is dependent on mobilizing constituencies in order to dominate the competition in a local power struggle.

> If multiple insurgent groups are competing for public support, bombings will intensify in both scope and number as they become both the litmus test of militancy and the way to mobilize greater numbers of people within their community. When competition is especially intense, multiple organizations have occasionally vied with

> one another to claim responsibility for a particular bombing and identify the bomber as their operative. Such spectacular 'heroic' attacks garner increased media attention and organizations vie to claim responsibility for martyrs. The more spectacular and daring the attacks, the more the insurgent organization is able to reap a public relations advantage over its rivals and/or enemies ... This process of outbidding between the groups depends on the domestic politics of the minority group and the state counter terror strategies and responses to insurgent violence.
>
> *(Bloom 2005: 77–78)*

Bloom is supported by Atran and by Gupta and Mundra. According to Atran, charismatic leaders of terrorist groups tend to manipulate the organization to achieve their desired political goals, therefore 'the key to understanding and parrying suicide terrorism is to concentrate more on the organizational structure, indoctrination methods, and ideological appeal of recruiting organizations' (Atran 2003: 13). Analysis by Gupta and Mundra of suicide bombings by Hamas and Islamic Jihad leads them to conclude that, contrary to the popular image of suicide terrorism as an outcome of irrational religious fanaticism, suicide attacks are part of an intensely political series of moves by the two groups (Gupta and Mundra 2005). They are produced within a complex cauldron of political calculations, where the major insurgent groups sometimes compete and sometimes co-operate with each other with the specific objective of increasing their base of support within the Palestinian community. 'These attacks are well timed strategic uses of human sacrifice for specific nationalistic and religious goals by the leadership of the dissident groups' (Gupta and Mundra 2005: 591). They also found that political provocations were the best predictor of future suicide attacks.

Analysis by Brym and Araj of Palestinian suicide bombings in the second intifada (2000–04) also offers partial support for the outbidding hypothesis. At the beginning of the second intifada in July 2000, almost four times more Palestinians supported Fatah than Hamas, 37 per cent versus 10 per cent respectively. Around the same time, 26 per cent of Palestinians supported suicide bombings. As Israel introduced more repressive policies, with strong resistance coming from Hamas, the support for suicide bombings soared to 66 per cent in December 2000, and support for Hamas began to increase while that for Fatah decreased. 'Thus, in the period July to December 2000, increasing support for suicide bombings was associated with falling support for Fatah and rising support for Hamas, as the outbidding thesis predicts' (Brym and Araj 2008: 497). However, they also point out that in the later stages of the second intifada, the outbidding hypothesis was inapplicable because it failed to account for variation in public support for suicide operations.

In general, Bloom's outbidding hypothesis is most persuasive in the Palestinian case. In the post-2000 Al-Aqsa intifada, the internal politics and competition among the three main Palestinian insurgent groups were dominant when secular and religious organizations competed for control over the Palestinian insurgency. But it is also well known that Palestinian factions co-operate as well as compete (Ricolfi 2005; Crenshaw 2007). Bloom's case study of Sri Lanka offers only partial support for her theory because, by the time LTTE began its suicide attacks in 1987, the other Tamil militant groups had largely been destroyed (Reuter 2004: 150; Pape 2005: 139). Following Bloom's framework, suicide attacks should have occurred between 1983 and 1987 when LTTE faced the most intense competition from its rivals. But the first suicide attack in Sri Lanka occurred in 1987 (Pedahzur 2005: 242).

The outbidding hypothesis does not appear to hold in Iraq either. While the Islamist insurgents and Baathists, who are most involved in suicide attacks in Iraq, are politically marginal and need extraordinary tactics to influence insurgency, their primary motivation is not to compete with other political factions. Their goal is to cause chaos and spark a sectarian civil war to hasten the collapse of the political system and create an environment conducive to their survival. Multitudes of groups involved in the Iraqi insurgency rarely compete with each other. Most of the insurgent groups have not adopted suicide attacks as a tactic in a consistent way to compete with Al-Qaeda In Iraq (AQI) and other groups that deploy suicide terrorism. Key to Bloom's escalatory dynamics is the diffusion of the tactics from one group to another. In the case of the Palestinians, the initial wave of suicide bombings by Hamas and Islamic Jihad prompted other secular groups, such as Al-Aqsa Martyrs Brigades and the Popular Front for the Liberation of Palestine (PFLP), to adopt this tactic. This contagion effect, generally speaking, has not taken place among the insurgent groups in Iraq (Hafez 2007b: 217).

The role of terrorist organizations has also been highlighted by the Israeli psychologist Ariel Merari, who has interviewed suicide bombers arrested before they could carry out their missions. In his evidence before a special committee of the US Congress on suicide terrorism, he rejected the notion that suicide bombers were crazy or that they carried out the attacks primarily for religious reasons:

> To put it in a nutshell, suicide terrorism is an organizational phenomenon ... it was an organization that decided to use this tactic, found the person or persons to carry it out, trained them, and sent them on the mission at the time and place that the organization chose.
>
> *(Merari 2000: 10)*

Palestinian groups put a great deal of effort into preparing and training potential suicide bombers, which was construed as brainwashing by the Israeli authorities and public. Merari rejects this construction. Once the organization decided that a certain person was suitable for the suicide mission, he/she was put through a training process that might last in most cases from weeks to months.

> This training process involves two important elements. One element is strengthening the already existing willingness to die by giving that person additional reasons ... in this phase of the training if the organization is religious the trainer also speaks about the religious justifications for this kind of act, about paradise, about the right or actually the need to carry out an act in the name of God, in the name of religion.
>
> *(Merari 2000: 12–13)*

The organization creates points of no return by having the bombers write last letters to their families and often also videotaping candidates saying farewell. In the Palestinian organizations, from this point onward the person is referred to as *alshahid al-hai*, 'the living martyr', meaning the individual is already dead and is only temporarily in this world. After this phase, it is very hard for a person to change their mind. Indeed, there have been practically no cases of changes of mind by suicide candidates in the case of Palestinians and very few in the case of Tamil Tigers and Hezbollah (Merari 2000; Silke 2003; Atran 2003). The existence of this strategy underlines the fact that the motivation to carry out an attack is not necessarily absolute.

In his study of suicide bombings in Iraq, Hafez combines elements from altruistic explanations and organizational strategies to develop a social movement theory of suicide terrorism (Hafez 2007b). Social movements are non-institutionalized, spontaneous social alliances of people protesting against widespread collective grievances. Hafez postulates that societies experiencing endemic, violent, asymmetrical conflicts involving state and non-state actors create opportunity structures to frame collective grievances as threats to identity and for articulating claims against the opponents. This framing forges networking among activists and their constituencies and creates individual motivations for volunteering for suicide bombings as a resistance strategy and its diffusion. He then uses this theory to explain suicide bombings in Iraq. Whereas Pape, Bloom and others take the sponsoring organizations and their strategic logic as given, Hafez offers an explanation of their emergence as social entities performing the functions and roles stipulated in his social organization theory. One can argue that social movement theory in fact strengthens the organizational logic and effectiveness perspectives rather than replacing them.

In conclusion, why do terrorist organizations engage in suicide violence? The studies summarized above would suggest that their decision to adopt this strategy is based on rational calculations. The organizations take decisions to maximise their ideological and political goals. Thus, adoption of this strategy reveals an organization's preference for maximising ideological aims as well as its need to compete for power and prestige within its constituency. More specifically, from the perspective of sponsoring organizations, suicide bombing attacks are motivated by (1) a carefully designed rational strategy of retaliatory actions by the weaker non-state actors facing well-armed states in an asymmetrical conflict in order to achieve their political goals; (2) efforts to achieve a competitive advantage for the sponsoring organization over its competitors for moral, material and human support in the sympathetic constituencies; and (3) a strategy designed to weaken or destroy the middle ground of compromise.

Societal conditions: repressive occupation, humiliation and altruism

If the perpetrators of suicide terror are not psychopaths or sociopaths, then how can we explain their destructive actions? The preceding section has provided an overview of the studies that explain suicide attacks as instrumental or strategic actions of sponsoring organizations engaged in asymmetrical conflicts with well equipped state armies. Suicide bombings mobilize support by responding to popular demand among sympathetic constituencies, which legitimizes the action and generates moral and material support for the organizations.

This section deals with studies and explanations that extend the scope of the analysis to societal conditions created by endemic conflicts characterized by oppressive policies and practices that cause widespread physical, economic, social and cultural dislocations. These dislocations undermine and even destroy the social bonds that glue the fabric of society, thus creating feelings of humiliation, resentment and revenge in the subject population. Sociologically, such conditions are conducive to the rise of altruism whereby some individual members are willing to sacrifice their lives for the honourable political survival of their community. Studies and explanations that are broadly grounded in this perspective will be discussed in this section. It begins with a brief overview of Durkheim's typology of suicide.

In his famous study of suicide more than half a century ago, Emile Durkheim brought together a number of insights to identify the areas and growing points of social dissolution in contemporary societies, putting these within a general theoretical framework which stated that suicide was related to the social integration of the individual's social group or society. 'Social integration' refers to the strength of the individual's ties to society and the stability of social relations within that society. In the lexicon of his theory, the relative degrees of integration, normlessness, social isolation and repression in society were the primary cause of the varying rates and types of suicide found in different societies (Durkheim 1951).

In Durkheim's typology, the most common type is 'egoistic suicide', caused by the individual's weak social integration in society leading to excessive isolation, which inhibits the individual's access to social support networks of family and religious community to help him or her cope with painful existential conditions. The mainspring of egoistic suicide is excessive individualism. The individual is like the protagonist in Sartre's *La Nausée*, a man with few social ties, all alone in his loneliness. Closely related to egoistic suicide is anomic suicide, which is caused by an abrupt change of circumstances, leading to 'social detachment'. The mechanisms leading to these two types of suicides are the same: personal trauma combined with social isolation. They differ only in the duration of detachment – chronic in egoistic suicide, acute in anomic. Another type of suicide in Durkheim's typology is fatalistic suicide, which is the converse of anomic suicide and occurs when the individual is subjected to oppressive and excessive regulation. The individual feels that he or she has no personal control or freedom and perceives the future to be relentlessly blocked and passions violently repressed by unavoidable and inflexible rules over which he or she feels powerless.

Durkheim identified a fourth type of suicide – altruistic suicide – in his aetiological typology. Unlike the anomic and egoistic types of suicides, which originate in extreme personal and social detachment, altruistic suicide emanates from the opposite condition: excessive integration of the individual into society. Altruism is to have the utmost, unselfish regard for others in society as a principle of action. One acts unselfishly on the basis of the rules, expectations and dictates of others in society. Altruism, for Durkheim, is where the ego is not its own property, where it is blended with something not itself, where the goal of conduct is exterior to itself, that is, in one of the groups in which it participates. Altruistic suicide occurs with the concurrence of circumstances in which:

> Either death had to be imposed by society as a duty, or some question of honour was involved, or at least some disagreeable occurrence had to lower the value of life in the victims' eyes. But it even happens that the individual kills himself purely for the joy of sacrifice, because, even with no particular reason, renunciation in itself is considered praiseworthy.
>
> *(Durkheim 1951: 223)*

Under conditions of intense attachment, society can exert pressure on the individual to make personal sacrifices, including sacrifice of his or her life as a validation of that attachment. Such action would confer prestige, public praise and recognition on the individual. Unwillingness to make the supreme sacrifice in such conditions would cost the individual public respect. Unlike egoistic, anomic or fatalistic suicides, altruistic suicide is likely to be a public act. Accordingly, the more a person values their community, the more likely he or she is to commit suicide for the sake of the community, 'because it is his duty' (Durkheim 1951: 219). The nature of altruistic suicide was summed up by Albert Camus in his essay *The Myth of Sisyphus*: 'What is called a reason for living is also an excellent reason for dying'.

The social construction of altruism

Human society is a living and vibrant organism integrated through a complex set of social networks grounded in historically generated cultural and social codes. It confers identities on its members, and its institutions invest these identities with meanings. When the social fabric of a society is threatened, it produces serious consequences ranging from political and social upheavals to emotional responses, including collective trauma, revenge, humiliation and rage – a kind of 'social pain'. These consequences are most visible in the 'war zones' of a society. The following is a description of the Sri Lankan situation.

> In the war zones, violence and war gradually permeated all aspect of daily life, family and community processes. It was not certain a person going for work would return in the evening. A home could be suddenly searched, someone brutally killed, a mother raped or father taken away. A shell could land anywhere destroying everything around. Sounds of gun shots, machine-gun fire, exploding shells, diving planes and rounding helicopters were present. People had to adapt to frequent checks, getting down from bikes, showing ID cards, waiting while military looked you over, body searches, the pushing and slaps, intimidation, women taking the sexual overtones and harassment as part of their daily ordeal all in the atmosphere of possible arrest. This kind of pervasive atmosphere of violence, rather than breaking down the resistance and spirit of the population, in time creates resistance and defiance, particularly in the youth. Thus within each breast would grow, small at first, a rage, hate which could transform into a militant. Thus these kinds of counter-insurgency policies and strategies would spawn a whole generation of rebellious youth.
>
> *(Nordstrom 1994, cited in Somasundaram 2008b)*

The counter-insurgency strategy of the Sri Lankan government against the Liberation Tigers of Tamil Eelam (LTTE) employed torture routinely.

Under the pretext of obtaining information, it was used to break the individual personalities of those who tried to resist, as well as being an encompassing method to coerce a community into submission. Many individuals did not survive torture; those who did were released in a broken condition, or, when dead, their maimed bodies were conspicuously exhibited to act as a warning to others. Thus, torture became an institutionalized aspect of state terror and a method of social control. Laws legitimizing torture and death in custody were passed. Similarly, torture was used by the militants but without any legal veneer (Doney 1998; Amnesty International 1986; Somasundaram 2008b). These conditions of sustained acute social and psychological trauma and chaos also created conditions for altruistic actions that attracted volunteers to LTTE and to the Black Tigers (LTTE's suicide squad). This is borne out by what little material exists on personal motivations for joining the Tamil Tigers. According to Father Harry Miller, a Jesuit priest who headed a Peace Committee at Batticaloa, in eastern Sri Lanka, 'The abuse that ordinary people suffer at the hands of the army becomes the primary motivating factor to join the Tigers' (Hopgood 2005: 70; Joshi 2000).

One of the most respected observers of the Sri Lankan situation, Peter Schalk, uses a 1993 LTTE-produced film to highlight the altruism behind a young Tamil's decision to join the Black Tigers. The film is called *Tayakkanava* or 'The Dream of the Motherland'. It spends a significant amount of time establishing the main character's motivation. It starts by showing a happy family consisting of parents, a daughter and a son, the *tiyaki* (martyr-to-be). They are all happy, sitting in a garden celebrating a birthday. They feed each other with their hands as a sign of intimacy. They also have good relations with their neighbours. The son takes a neighbour's young daughter to school on his motorbike. One day the Sri Lankan air force drops bombs on the school, and the boy can only take the body of his young friend to her parents. In his inner vision, he perceives that this could have happened to his own younger sister, and he decides he will enter the squad of Black Tigers, having obtained his father's permission. The film shows the hard training given to a Black Tiger and spends much time describing the comradeship that develops within the group, especially between our hero and his comrades. One day he is selected for a vehicle-borne suicide mission. Before going on the mission, he divides his property between his comrades and bids farewell to his family and finally to the

LTTE leader, Prabhakaran. The following day, the mission is carried out as planned. The enemy camp is eliminated, and he is killed. The next day, all read and talk about him. His picture is put up on a commemorative altar. Then his parents are informed by two officials from LTTE that he has reached *viramaranam*, 'heroic death' (Schalk 1997b, quoted in Hopgood 2005).

The above account, although fictional, is a good description of the reality on the ground. It shows that the social construction of the altruistic martyrdom of Tamil Tigers is well supported by the Tamil population of Sri Lanka. Since the mid-1990s, all observers to Tamil-held areas of Jaffna, the LTTE stronghold in the northern region of the country, have reported strong support for suicide operations and commemoration of the LTTE martyrs among the local population. Each year on 5 July, thousands attend the 'Heroes' Day' celebration, commemorating the first Black Tiger, whose mission occurred on 5 July 1987, and others since. There are also hundreds of shrines to individual suicide attackers, kept with flowers and with special trees planted to represent the martyrs who 'planted' their lives for the land. Although the LTTE were routed by the Sri Lankan army in early 2009, while they ruled the Jaffna peninsula they contributed to the social and economic life of the local society by devoting the group's limited resources to social services. LTTE was the only insurgent group in the world that ran a *de facto* state within a state for almost twenty years. LTTE provided thousands of people with all the social, health, economic, judicial and security services normally provided by the state as well as with interest-free loans. In 1993, the Tigers established Tamil Eelam Bank to help local small businesses to stimulate the local economy (Hopgood 2005; Bloom 2005; Roberts 2007, 2008).

The LTTE's discourse on martyrdom emphasizes the altruistic motives and instrumental value of self-sacrifice to liberate the Tamil 'homeland' from Sinhalese occupation. According to the LTTE leader, Prabhakaran, 'our martyrs die in the arena of struggle with the intense passion for the freedom of their people, for the liberation of their homeland and therefore the death of every martyr constitutes a brave act of enunciation of freedom' (Prabhakaran 1993). Black Tigers seek to overcome conventional inferiority to the Sri Lankan army through self-sacrifice.

According to a female LTTE fighter, Nandani:

> As Black Tigers, they are a physical embodiment of self-determination and liberation. They employ their lives as missiles armed with

> the kind of determination and purpose that is unmatched by any conventional weapon that the Sinhala forces may deploy. There lies the strength and honor of our Black Tigers.
>
> *(Pape 2005: 194)*

In the thirty years of its existence, the LTTE has succeeded in building strong bonds with the local Tamil community, creating opportunities for individuals willing to sacrifice for the community through suicide attacks. A study of LTTE describes this support in the following words:

> Why does the LTTE have so much support among the population? It is the only group that is accepted by the population as 'one of our own', 'our boys', even 'our sons' ... The LTTE are the one militant group that has managed to build up grassroots support and loyalty among the population for reasons both ideological and organizational and got a grip on the political and social structure of Jaffna.
>
> *(Hellmann-Rajanayagam 1994, cited in Pape 2005: 195)*

After an extensive analysis of suicides in the modern world informed by Durkheim's typology, Pape concludes: 'Overall, egoistic and anomic motives are insufficient to account for the individual logic of suicide terrorism. Altruistic motives, either alone or in conjunction with others, likely play an important role' (Pape 2005: 184). Virtually all ordinary suicides are the private acts of solitary individuals. Suicide bombings, on the other hand, are always public acts, and a large proportion are either team attacks or part of joint missions against the same target or targets in close proximity, indicating the presence of altruistic motives among many suicide attackers. This does not preclude the existence of a personal motive to die, but suicide attackers who work together in teams must also be motivated to achieve a collective purpose, the completion of a group mission that serves a cause beyond their own personal death. This, of course, does not imply that single-person suicide missions do not involve altruistic motives. Martyrs' videos and other last testaments often claim that the suicide attack was motivated by altruism. The existence of team attack as well as martyr videos and other testaments left by individuals suggests that most suicide terrorists are motivated partly or wholly by a collective purpose and not by personal anguish and pain (Pape 2005: 186–87; Orbach 2004; Reuter 2004; Oliver and Steinberg 2005; Dabbagh 2005).

Almost all terrorist organizations sponsoring suicide bombings are bound to their societies by virtue of pursuing political goals seen as legitimate by the society at large, and by their participation in extensive networks of social services and charities for the benefit of the society. They are also involved in elaborate ceremonies and rituals that identify the death of a suicide bomber with the good of the community. This is evident from the activities and organizational structures of Hezbollah, Hamas, the Liberation Tigers of Tamil Eelam and Lashkar-e-Toiba. The purpose of such activities is to demonstrate to the community that the sacrifice and martyrdom of suicide attackers is justified by its instrumental value in protecting the community from foreign occupation and is not an end in itself. The survival of the community, they argue, demands self-sacrifice. Hezbollah, Hamas, LTTE, Laskar-e-Toiba, Taliban, Ansar al-Islam, Mujahidin Shura Council, Al Qaeda and AQI all claim that the purpose of suicide missions is to end foreign occupation of the 'homeland'. From the point of view of these organizations, suicide missions are needed because of the imbalance in conventional military power between the combatants; moreover, the suicide mission will put coercive pressure on the enemy to make concessions. In other words, suicide missions are framed in altruistic terms not as an end in themselves but as a means of achieving multiple ends for the good of the community.

In short, under conditions of massive disruption in society, altruism and altruistic motives can be cultivated to garner support for suicide bombing. Communities that have endured a long and painful conflict with a more powerful enemy eventually react to perceived inferiority and the failure of other efforts by supporting suicide attacks. Religiously coded attitudes towards the acceptance of death stemming from long periods of hopelessness and suffering enable political organizations to give people suicide bombing as an outlet for expressing feelings of deprivation, injustice, despair and hostility. Paradoxically, an enemy's brutal response reinforces these feelings (Pedahzur 2005; Pedahzur and Perliger 2006; Pape 2005; Hafez 2006, 2007b; Atran 2003; N. Hassan 2001).

An investigation of the role of altruistic motivation in the Palestinian territories shows that suicide terrorism was an outcome of altruistic and fatalistic motivations. Countering some popular depictions of suicide bombers as unsophisticated young men who either were artfully recruited or became suicide bombers at the instigation of charismatic imams (mosque prayer leaders), the study found that conditions in the Palestinian territories were such that the would-be martyr's decision to embark on his or her journey of destruction was reinforced by the approval of the community and concern for its honourable survival. The tendency of terrorists to offer themselves for suicide missions was a result not just of operational and organizational advantages but also of individuals' strong affinity with the goals and values of their society. Two main factors influencing the decision to become a suicide terrorist were a desire to help Palestinian society achieve its political goals and a desire to escape from a hopeless situation that prevailed in Palestinian society (Pedahzur, Perliger and Weinberg 2003). The influence of these and other similar factors help to motivate angry young Palestinian men and women to transform themselves into heroes and heroines. Their lethal actions become models of self-sacrifice and total commitment of true believers to the cause of the oppressed. 'That message is sent loud and clear to the next cadre of young suicide bombers in waiting' (Zimbardo 2007: 292).

The French film-maker Pierre Rehov interviewed many Palestinians in Israeli jails who had been arrested following their failed suicide bombing missions or for aiding and abetting such missions for his film *Suicide Killers*. Every single one of them tried to convince him that that suicide bombing was the right thing to do for moralistic reasons. According to Rehove, 'These aren't kids who want to do evil. These are kids who want to do good ... The result of this brainwashing was kids who were very good people inside [were] believing so much that they were doing something great' (Curiel 2006). The experience of the everyday degradations of Israeli occupation had created collective hatred in them which made them susceptible to indoctrination to become youthful living martyrs. 'It is neither mindless nor senseless, only a very different mind-set and with different sensibilities than we have been used to witnessing among young adults in most countries' (Zimbardo 2007: 292).

Studies of the social and political consequences of Israeli occupation on Palestinian society have found that the conditions of the occupation were a significant cause of suicide bombings in the Palestinian–Israeli conflict. Findings of a recent study of this problem indicate that state repression in conflicts where suicide bombing has been used should not be perceived only as reaction to the bombings: it often precedes and is a major cause of such attacks. Harsh repression at the micro-level was found to be a major contributor to the rise in suicide bombings. The study found that revenge for Israeli actions against the bomber, his/her family or friends or Palestinians in general was the main motivation for the majority of the bombers in the second intifada. In addition, public support turned individual bombers into heroes and thus encouraged more volunteers. Without individuals, organizations cannot conduct their suicide attacks, and without enough volunteers, suicide 'campaigns' are not possible. In a society characterized by strong social solidarity, individual members are prone to altruistic suicides in an attempt to achieve collective political goals (Araj 2008: 66–67). A strong relationship between repression and collective action in Palestine was also identified by Khawaja, who found that, instead of deterring protest, repression increased subsequent collective action. Provocations or violations of 'honour' and established moral codes induce people to adopt a confrontational stance towards authorities and turn them into supporters of the collective cause (Khawaja 1993).

These findings are echoed in another study of Palestinian resistance and suicide bombings, which found that the main motivations for acts of self-sacrifice by young Palestinians lay in the heavy repression of Israeli occupation experienced in everyday Palestinian life. The martyrdom operations in the form of 'intelligent human bombs' represented a tactic utilized in asymmetrical warfare in an attempt to match superior Israeli military power and to shake Israeli society and morale. The misery and personal traumas arising from a brutalizing occupation created an immense anger, bitterness and hatred that justified the extreme response. For Palestinians, suicide bombings were acts of ultimate despair, horrific reactions to extremely inhumane conditions in a seriously damaged environment of hopelessness (Ahmed 2005).

A collective sense of unjust persecution can quickly build up in aggrieved communities and creates a sense of moral outrage that provides the motivation as well as justification for extreme violence. Interviewed in prison, one Palestinian terrorist expressed his sense of outrage to two Israeli academics in the following words:

> You Israeli are Nazis in your souls and in your conduct. In your occupation you never distinguish between men and women, or

> between old people and children. You adopted methods of collective punishment, you uprooted people from their homeland and from their homes and chased them into exile. You fired live ammunition at women and children. You smashed the skulls of defenceless civilians. You set up detention camps for thousands of people in sub-human conditions. You destroyed homes and turned children into orphans. You prevented people from making a living, you stole their property, you trampled on their honour. Given that kind of conduct, there is no choice but to strike at you without mercy in every possible way.
>
> *(Post and Denny 2002)*

Suicide bombing is a new phenomenon in Palestinian society. Palestinian psychiatrist El Sarraj attributes its rise to the hopelessness that comes from a situation that continues to worsen: a despair where living becomes no different from dying propels people to unthinkable actions (El Sarraj 2002). Life under occupation is psychologically traumatic and becomes one continuous experience of humiliation for Palestinians:

> [Palestinians] need to feel respected. They want status within their society. Today the martyr is glorified. The martyr for them is the power of the people, the power to take revenge on behalf of the victims ... They see a martyr as courageously sacrificing himself or herself for the sake of everyone, as a symbol of the struggle for freedom, because this is what these people are fighting for.
>
> *(Butler 2002: 72)*

A number of studies claim that Hamas used the Islamic concept of jihad to frame suicide attacks as martyrdom operations, a concept that had not been formulated in these terms previously in Palestinian society. Palestinians have come to venerate martyrdom because of a confluence of perceived threats and a sense of victimization. The public sought both revenge and empowerment in response to harsh Israeli occupation and actions. Islam presented a cultural and theological rationalization for framing suicide operations as martyrdom, but the failure of secular Palestinian Authority leaders to counter or condemn such constructions allowed Hamas and Palestinian Islamic Jihad the political opening they sought. The sponsoring organization can mobilize altruistic support for suicide attacks using not only religion but also nationalism enhanced by resentment of foreign occupation, the repressive and brutal policies of the occupying force, long periods of occupation, the severity of conflicts, civilian casualties, as well as failure effectively to counter the tactics and failure of alternatives (Hafez 2006; Khosrokhavar 2005; Crenshaw 2007; El Sarraj 2002; Margalit 2003; Pape 2005; Bloom 2005; Pedahzur 2005).

Recent studies about pathways to extremist violence and terrorism by Scott Atran and his colleagues show that today's most virulent terrorism is rooted in rootlessness and restlessness, not in the clash of civilizations along traditional historical faultlines but in a crash of traditional territorial cultures. Individuals in the modern world are mostly radicalized horizontally with their peers, rather than vertically through institutional leaders or organizational hierarchies. In particular, what inspires young people to get involved in lethal terrorist actions is not so much the Koran or religious teachings as a thrilling cause and call to action that promises glory and esteem in the eyes of friends as well as eternal respect and remembrance in the wider community that they will never live to enjoy. In the Muslim world, most young people who join the jihad have had a moderate and mostly secular education rather then a radical, religious one. Many who are bored, underemployed, overqualified and underwhelmed by hopes for the future turn to jihad with their friends. The watchwords for many are 'jihad' and 'change'. They constantly see and discuss among themselves images of war and injustice against 'our people', becoming morally outraged if injustice resonates personally in their families' and community's lives (Atran 2010; ARTIS 2009).

In short, altruistic motives are significant in explaining the moral logic of suicide missions. By their very nature, suicide missions involve collective motives and are sponsored by organizations that go to great lengths to embed themselves in the surrounding communities and pursue socially acceptable political objectives. Through their political and social activities, these organizations create altruistic conditions and opportunities for their members to volunteer to sacrifice for the community if they wish to do so. The individual may be driven to self-sacrifice by social and psychological traumas arising from the conditions of the war zone and/or the absence of recourse to solutions to perceived injustices. Under such conditions, feelings of rage and revenge act as the means to set the scales of justice right.

The individuals who wish to sacrifice for their community can be confident that the act is understood as such. The weight of existing evidence suggests that self destruction can be actively induced by society and does not grow exclusively out of personal anguish and pain (Orbach 2004; Pape 2005; Hafez 2007b; Gambetta 2005; Bloom 2005; Battin 2004; Abdel-Khalek 2004).

In conclusion, this review reveals a multitude of explanations of suicide bombing and little consensus on its conceptualization, causes and consequences. Studies that focus on explaining the phenomenon in terms of individualistic motivations conceptualize suicide bombings as acts of abhorrent illegal violence against civilians perpetrated by psychopaths and sociopaths. Studies seeking to develop social and psychological profiles of the perpetrators of suicide bombing have not produced much in the way of fruitful results and have failed to find a stable set of demographic, socio-economic, religious and psychological variables that can be causally linked to the suicide bomber's personality. Results of studies of commonly held stereotypes, especially among politicians and even among some scholars, that see the root cause of suicide terrorism as social and economic deprivation have found no correlation between poverty and suicide terrorism. In fact, the evidence shows that, conversely, a higher standard of living is positively associated with support for or participation in terrorism. Still, this line of inquiry remains attractive among scholars around the world. Labels like mad, bad, fanatics, homicidal killers and insane may serve a useful function for legal purposes, but if the purpose of studies is to learn and understand the causes of suicide terrorism and the means by which it can be prevented, then these labels simply hinder us from discovering its real nature, purpose and causes.

On the other hand, studies of the role, function and nature of terrorist organizations and altruistic motives as the driving force behind suicide bombings provide holistic and rounded explanations. In general, they show that suicide bombings are a weapon of the weaker non-state entity engaged in asymmetrical conflicts with well-armed state armies. The conflict invariably involves liberation of the homeland. The non-state organizations employ suicide attacks in order to mobilize support among sympathetic constituencies. Suicide attacks have symbolic and instrumental values: they mobilize moral and material support and at the same time respond to popular demands. The ultimate goals are political and not religious, but religion can mobilize both support and participation because of its emphasis on redemption and martyrdom. Individuals may be driven to self-sacrifice by a cocktail of emotions including pride, honour, anger, rage, humiliation, shame, powerlessness and hopelessness.

Suicide bombings benefit the sponsoring organization in two ways: by coercing an adversary and by giving the sponsoring organization an advantage over its rival in terms of support from sympathetic constituencies. But these claims are assertions and not always supported by evidence. Sponsoring organizations go to great lengths to embed themselves in their communities in order to pursue socially acceptable political goals. By pursuing their political goals they create altruistic conditions for individuals to volunteer to sacrifice for their community.

4

SUICIDE BOMBINGS

Homicidal killing or a weapon of war?

The eminent US political theorist Michael Walzer describes suicide bombings and terrorism as homicidal killing and morally worse than killing in war: 'Terrorists are killers on a rampage, except that rampage is not just expressive of rage or madness: the rage is purposeful and programmatic ... the peculiar evil of terrorism is not only the killing of innocent people but also the intrusion of fear into everyday life, the violation of private purposes, the insecurity of public spaces, the endless coerciveness of precaution' (Walzer 2004, 2006). Walzer's writings have been very influential in shaping the debate of the suicide bombings and bombers in the media.

This chapter will examine whether suicide bombings are homicidal killing, as argued by Walzer, or a weapon of war. This examination will involve exploration of several interrelated questions: Is suicidal bombing a form of suicidal behaviour? If not, then should it be viewed as an act of murder or a weapon of war? To establish this we must also ascertain the nature of war and killing in war, and distinguish war killing from murder. The answers to these questions would help to answer the question of whether suicide bombing is homicidal killing or a weapon of war. These questions are explored in the following discussion.

Suicide and suicide bombing

There is an emerging consensus among scholars that suicide attacks are qualitatively different from suicides. After a comprehensive of review of relevant literature on the phenomenon of suicide bombing, Grimland, Apter and Kerkhof (2006) conclude that social factors such as group dynamics, indoctrination and political circumstances are decisive in analysing this problem. They assert that in suicidal bombing, suicide is instrumental in the context of war, not in the context of psychopathology. The act of killing in warfare is more important to understanding suicidal terrorism than the act of suicide.

In another comprehensive review of the topic, Townsend concludes that suicide terrorism has a range of characteristics which, on close examination, are shown to be different from other suicidal behaviour. 'Suicide terrorists are not truly suicidal and attempting to find commonalities between suicide terrorists and others who die by suicide is likely to be an unhelpful path for any discipline wishing to further understanding of suicidal behaviour. Equating actions and motivations of suicide terrorists with those of other suicides perhaps does something of a disservice to those individuals who die quietly, alone and with no murderous intent' (Townsend 2007: 47).

The British–Palestinian psychiatrist Nadia Dabbagh (2005) in her study of suicide in Palestine shows that suicidal behaviour in Palestinian society, like suicide in other societies, is caused by the relative degree of social integration, regulation and isolation, as well as by social and cultural control and oppression of individuals in society. But suicide bombings by organizations such as Hamas and Islamic Jihad are targeted acts of resistance and weapons of the weak against an unjust and hated occupier of what the Palestinians regard as their homeland.

Unlike suicide, which evokes feelings of pity and sadness for the victims, suicide attacks evoke emotions of repulsion, fear, anger and total disbelief that a human being can kill, in such a cold-blooded manner, innocent people who have done no harm to the perpetrator. The main difference between suicide bombing attacks and suicides is that in suicide bombing the primary intention of the act is murder, whereas a primary characteristic of suicide is the absence of murderous intent. In fact, the terrorist's suicide can be viewed as a by-product of the attack. Typically, suicide attacks involve victims who are unknown to the killer. Moreover, most suicide attacks are carefully planned well in advance, with the explicit intention of killing others who have no prior relationship with the suicide bomber (Dabbagh 2005; Townsend 2007). Suicide bombing attacks are also different from homicide-suicide because of the temporal spacing of the acts of homicide and suicide. In suicide bombing the acts are simultaneous (Marzuk, Tardiff and Hirsch 1992; Barraclough and Harris 2002; Townsend 2007)

War and war killing

According to ethnographic evidence war, which can be defined as organized lethal violence involving spatially and socially distinct groups, is caused by economic factors (land, resources and plunder), social factors (prestige, honour), revenge (for sufferings) and defence. The order of motives from most inclusive to least inclusive are: political control, economic gain, social status and defence (Wright 1942; Otterbein 1970). Motives for going to war appear to differ according to the nature of the political system. Centralized political systems (states and chiefdoms) go to war for the purposes of conquering, dominating and achieving political control over a territory and its inhabitants in order to extract economic benefits. In contrast, tribes, bands and non-state groups do not make war to attain political control but for a combination of purposes, which may include revenge, defence, land, honour and prestige (Kelly 2000).

In modern political theory, war is organized violence and an instrument of the state. It is a legal activity when it fulfils certain conditions such as self-defence or the upholding of a treaty obligation toward a state that is being attacked, or constitutes a humanitarian intervention to safeguard the existence of a political community threatened with either the elimination of its people or the coercive transformation of their way of life. Neither of these actions is morally acceptable. Under these conditions, war is legal and justifiable, but only as a method of last resort after all alternatives have been exhausted. Additionally, the conduct of war is always subject to moral criticism and must not directly target civilians and economic infrastructures and must be proportional (Walzer 2004: 45).

These criteria give legitimacy to certain types of violence and stigmatize other types under international law. But, as Talal Asad has argued, the irony of the liberal West's culture of war is the coexistence of, on the one hand, the state's need to legitimize organized violence against a collective enemy (including civilians) and, on the other hand, the humanitarian desire to save human lives (Asad 2007: 16). While both war and terrorism are explicit forms of death dealing, these criteria make killing in war legitimate and killing by terrorism illegal. (Walzer 2004: 51)

Much of the criticism of terrorism follows on from these fundamental precepts of war in political theory. In war and terrorism, innocents are killed but what liberal political theory condemns in war is *excess* and in terrorism its *essence*. But whether state armies kill only those who are legitimately killable is partly what the rules of war address (Asad 2007: 16). While war, according to Walzer, is the method of last resort, the militants carrying out acts of terrorism against civilians have not been through the necessary steps to justify their actions as being a last resort and are thus not coerced into that action. In his eyes, it is not so easy to reach the last resort. To get there one must indeed try everything, and not just once but repeatedly; politics, after all, is an art of repetition (Walzer 2004: 53).

In short, war, an organized violence in which death of the 'other' is encoded in the planning, is the legitimate and legal prerogative of the state under certain conditions. Its legitimacy is grounded in the exclusive power of the state to impose punishments internally and externally. Violence is embedded, therefore, in the very concept of liberty which is at the heart of liberal doctrine about the foundation of the political community which the state is empowered to defend. The concept presupposes that the morally independent individual's natural right to violent self-defence is yielded to the state and that the state becomes the sole protector of individual liberties, denying to any agents other than the state the right to kill at home and abroad (Tuck 1999). The right to kill is the right to behave in violent ways against citizens who break the original covenant as well as against the uncivilized 'others' who pose a threat to the existence of civilized order, and their killing provides security. This is done in the name of self-defence. The justifications of pre-emptive and preventative wars (like the ones in Iraq and Afghanistan) practised by the modern state are embedded in this doctrine.

The doctrine of moral legitimacy and legality of war stipulates that the state is coerced into taking this action as the method of last resort after all alternatives have been exhausted. Furthermore, the state armies engaged in war do not target civilian non-combatants. Does this logic of war also apply to terrorists insurgencies involved in suicide bombings? The following two case studies, one from Palestinian and the other from Sri Lankan terrorist organizations, may help us to answer this question.

Palestine: In the case of Palestine, terrorist organizations employing suicide bombings claim to be involved in retaliatory violence in order to defend their *'political community'* whose very survival is being threatened by Israeli occupation and expansion. The continuation of this occupation and expansion would inevitably lead to the dispossession of the Palestinian homeland, amounting to the elimination of the Palestinians as a people and of their way of life. The Palestinian terrorist organizations claim they are engaged in organized violence through suicide bombings only as a last resort and under absolute necessity.

For most Palestinians, violence is their only option to achieve their goal of an independent state. A Palestinian recruiter and trainer of suicide bombers is quoted as saying, 'Jihad and resistance begin with the word, then with sword, then with the stone, then with the gun, then with planting bombs, then transforming bodies into human bombs' (Bloom 2005: 27). The pervasive sense of powerlessness among the Palestinians has made violence an all-powerful symbol of honour. At a profoundly symbolic level, martyrdom is the final and irrefutable statement of group worth and dignity against what is seen by the Palestinians as an oppressive Israeli occupation. According to the late Hamas leader Dr. Abdul Aziz Rantisi, a casualty of Israel's policy of targeted killing of Palestinian terrorist leaders, Hamas and Palestinian society in general believe that 'becoming a martyr through suicide bombing is among the highest if not the highest, honour' (Argo 2003: 17). As regards civilian deaths from Palestinian suicide bombings, there appears to be little concern over civilian immunity. For most Palestinians, there is no such thing as civilian immunity in Israel due to the universal conscription of men and women. Any civilian is either a current, past, or future soldier. From this perspective, all Israelis are complicit in the immoral and illegal occupation of the West Bank and Gaza (Bloom 2005: 40).

Finally, suicide bombing is only one of the weapons used by the three Palestinian organizations engaged in suicide bombings against Israel – Hamas, Palestinian Islamic Jihad and the Al-Aqsa Martyrs Brigades. These organizations have deep-rooted mass support in Palestinian society. Their violent confrontations with Israeli occupying forces are well organized and this applies especially to their suicide bombing operations which are well planned before they are executed. Taking this factor into account, it would appear that Palestinian violence against Israel meets most if not all the attributes of war except one: it is not carried out on behalf of a state but on behalf of a 'political community' which perceives its very existence and way of life under threat from Israeli occupation. Using Walzer's terminology, the Palestinian leaders confronted with a potential evil respond by doing evil for the protection of their political community (Walzer 2004).

The two most common explanations of Palestinian suicide bombings are as follows: (1) they are acts of religiously motivated sacrifice in the form of a martyrdom operation, and (2) they are acts of 'secular immortality'. They represent opposite ends of the sacred-profane continuum. An eloquent exposition of the first explanation is to be found in the work of Ivan Strenski. Drawing on the work of the Durkheimian school, he proposes that the phenomenon of suicide bombings is better understood through religious concepts of sacrifice and gift than through theories seeking to explain it as suicide. Sacrifice is not just a social deed but has a potent religious resonance that transforms it into something holy. In suicide bombing, Strenski argues, sacrifice of oneself is made as a gift to and for the nation or political community that sanctifies it. All Palestinian suicide bombers believe they are giving their lives for the Palestinian nation. Strenski's analysis thus implies that since sacrifice is the essence of religious subjectivity, violence is integral to it (Strenski 2003).

One can take issue on at least two fronts with Strenski's description of suicide bombing. Firstly, his argument is actually contrary to Durkheim's position. Durkheim was the first theorist to identify the social determinants of suicide and he would most certainly have classified suicide bombing within the category of altruistic suicide. Secondly, his description of the motive in terms of sacrifice offers a religious model by means of which suicide bombings can be identified as 'religious terrorism'. That appellation defines the bomber as morally underdeveloped – and therefore premodern – when compared with people whose civilized status is partly indicated by their secular politics and their private religion and whose violence is therefore in principle *disciplined, reasonable, and just* (Asad 2007: 45).

The second explanation, describing Palestinian suicide bombings as acts of secular immortality, has been offered by May Jayyusi and links different types of violent acts as manifestations of different kinds of subjectivities. Jayyusi links Palestinian suicide bombing to a particular type of political subjectivity formed in the context of their relationship to particular power structures. Drawing from Carl Schmitt's idea of 'the state of exception' and Georgio Agamben's Homo Sacer, she concentrates on developing a larger politico-ideological field which includes Israeli policies of occupation and settlements, the Palestinian resistance and international developments such as the Iranian Revolution and the Oslo Accord.

Jayyusi argues that the Oslo Accord was an attempt to institute a local authority over the Palestinians on behalf of the occupying Israeli state. Under the Oslo Accord, the entire Palestinian population was held hostage to the policing performance of the Palestinian Authority. As the overarching state power, Israel was at once beyond the Palestinian zones and yet sovereign over them. As a result, the Palestinian Authority was caught under these conditions in an irresolvable contradiction: on the one hand, it was seeking national sovereignty and on the other, it was conceding it indefinitely to the occupying power by agreeing unconditionally to carry out its policing function. In this power arrangement, something new emerged with the Oslo Accord for the Palestinian population, something Jayyusi calls 'an imaginary of freedom' (Jayyusi 2004).

This imaginary of freedom made the Oslo Accord acceptable to the Palestinians in spite of the misgivings of many and resulted in a significant decline in support for militant Islamic movements. In 1999, over 70 per cent of Palestinians supported the Palestinian Authority-led peace process and support for suicide bombings declined to 20 per cent. By 2003–04, as it became clear that the inherent contradictions of Oslo would not produce conditions of Palestinian liberation from Israeli occupation, paradoxically increasing the daily humiliation of Palestinians at Israeli army check points and not stopping the expansion of the Jewish settlements, the attitudes towards the Palestinian Authority shifted dramatically. The Palestinian Authority was seen as unable to stand up to Israeli power and its support among Palestinians plummeted to 22 per cent while support for suicide bombings increased to 75 per cent (Bloom 2005).

The consequence was a sense of outrage among Palestinians because Oslo had created the hope that conditions would change but they never did. Their rage was the consequence of this blocking of the legal, political means of their liberation. As Hannah Arendt (1969) has pointed out, when legal political means are blocked, the possibility of acting politically, which is part of what makes men individual and therefore human, is also blocked. That rage led to an action which offers them a secular form of immortality.

The phenomenon of Palestinian suicide bombing is thus an expression of that secular immortality and not of religious zealotry.

Sri Lanka: The ethnic antagonisms which arose over the Sri Lankan Tamil minority's agitation for economic, social and cultural equality gradually gave rise to Sinhalese nationalism and Tamil ethnic chauvinism soon after Sri Lanka gained its independence. Sinhalese nationalists denied the multi-ethnic and multi-religious character of Sri Lankan society and refused to accept the collective rights of minority groups. This discrimination became institutionalized in the new Constitution in the 1960s which excluded Tamils from government and other positions of authority, reducing their recruitment in government jobs from 41 per cent in 1949 to 7 per cent in 1963 while increasing Sinhalese proportions in the same period from 54 per cent to 92 per cent. A quota system was also imposed on Tamil students entering the universities.

The Tamils responded politically through the Federal Party and through non-violent protests called Satyagraha, but these efforts failed to lead to their demands being met. By the 1970s, Tamils had started to agitate for a separate homeland and their protestations became increasingly violent. In the 1980s, they won some concessions and political rights but discrimination remained palpable. Among the organizations which emerged in this period was a radical group called the Tamil National Tigers under the leadership of Vellupillai Prabhakaran, later renamed the Liberation Tigers of Tamil Eelam (LTTE). The main aim of the LTTE was the establishment of a Tamil homeland in the northern and eastern provinces of Sri Lanka.

The Sri Lankan government reacted to increasing Tamil militancy by promulgating the Prevention of Terrorism Act (PTA) in 1979. However, instead of mitigating violence, the PTA brought about the escalation of Tamil violence in the 1980s. The government responded in turn with additional repressive counter measures that led to a spiral of increasing brutality and tit-for-tat violence. In response to the murder of one of their commanders, LTTE operatives ambushed an army convoy in Jaffna, killing 13 Sinhalese soldiers in Jaffna and triggering widespread mob violence in which hundreds of Tamils died. New emergency regulations gave sweeping powers to security forces to kill and bury suspected terrorists without any judicial inquiries. The LTTE called these developments a pogrom against Tamils. After the riots, the government banned the main Tamil political party pushing Tamils to the LTTE as their main voice.

The Tamil insurgency arose after the failure of other forms of political struggle. The powerful Sri Lankan state, dominated by the Sinhalese majority, employed the army to oppress the Tamil community. Gradually the traditional 'homelands' of the Tamil minority became the 'war zones' in which life became increasingly harsh, unbearable and violent. This gave rise to a widespread perception among the Tamils that their very existence as a distinct ethnic and cultural community was being threatened. The LTTE began to employ suicide bombings effectively from 1987 in response to these developments and as a method of last resort. Although the LTTE was finally defeated in early 2009 by the Sri Lankan army, its defeat has not discredited the ideology which gave rise to the Tamil insurgency.

*

These case studies demonstrate that the violence of suicide bombings was the method of last resort in both Palestine and Sri Lanka. Using indicators of what constitutes war from the above two case studies, we can infer that the LTTE and Palestinian terrorist organizations using suicide bombings in their violent conflicts with the Sri Lankan and Israeli states respectively are engaged in organized violence akin to war. The objective in both cases is the protection of a political community and its way of life which faces mortal threat from its adversary. In both cases, the violence is organized and planned such that the death of the enemy is encoded. Suicide bombings in these organized violent conflicts are employed as a weapon of war by the militarily challenged, and thus the resulting deaths of the combatants and civilians are akin to the casualties of war.

Surprisingly, in the case of war, Walzer does not apply the same stringent conditions to the state as he imposes on terrorists. Modern states have a far greater capacity and capability to kill and destroy human lives than any terrorist organization in the world, an example being the aerial bombing of German civilians by the Allied air force during World War II. However, Walzer argues, this was a legitimate course of action whereas suicide bombing is terrorism. Moreover, as terrorism, suicide bombing is an evil in need not of analysis and understanding but of moral condemnation and firm practical response.

Walzer believes that suicide bombings in Israel are immoral and evil because they are part of the Palestinian mission to destroy a sovereign political community. The assaults of the Israeli army and air force in the

West Bank and Gaza are, therefore, pre-emptive self-defence and thus legitimate and justifiable. (By this logic, the Sri Lankan army's attacks on the Tamils are also legitimate and justifiable). The construction of the Israeli–Palestinian conflict in these terms is a typical example of how liberal intellectuals conceive of the difference between war and terrorism. The century-long history of the conflict, involving expansion on the one side and dispossession on the other, is set aside, and attention is directed instead at present feelings. For all their military strength, Israelis are portrayed as vulnerable while for the Palestinians the years of occupation have been years of disgrace (Asad 2007).

This construction also invests the Israeli and Sri Lankan armies with the aura of defenders engaged in a just war against Palestinian and Sri Lankan suicide bombers. The principle that a political community experiencing fatal attacks and facing 'the coercive transformation of their way of life' has the right to defend itself does not appear to apply to the Palestinian and Tamil responses. Their resistance is perceived as engagement in morally unacceptable violence, presumably because, even after fifty years (and in the case of Palestinians, even longer), of unequal struggle, they are not judged to have reached the state of the 'last resort'.

Killing in war and terrorism

As mentioned earlier, the difference between war killing and suicide bombing is that war is a legally sanctioned act which confers legitimacy on the ensuing killing whereas the killing perpetrated by unlicensed illegal terrorists is not legitimate. But what about the soldiers who are also taught to hate the enemy they are required to kill? The concept of killing being legally sanctioned is an abstract irrelevance. There are, in fact, remarkable similarities between war killing and terrorism.

Every war requires making the human killing machine efficient and effective. According to historian Joanne Bourke, basic military training is aimed at making soldiers extremely brutal:

> The most notorious training regimes were those conducted by the U.S. Marine Corps, but even in the other branches of the armed forces, violence was a common component of military training. In all these training programmes, the fundamental process was the

> same: individuals had to be broken down to be rebuilt into efficient fighting men. The basic tenets included depersonalization, uniforms, lack of privacy, forced social relationships, tight schedules, lack of sleep, disorientation followed by rites or reorganization according to military codes, arbitrary rules, and strict punishment. These methods of brutalization were similar to those carried out in regimes where men were taught to torture prisoners: the difference resided in the degree of violence involved, not its nature.
>
> *(Bourke 1999: 67)*

Another account provided by Nordstrom (2004: 71–72) describes the atrocities inflicted on civilians by the Sri Lankan soldiers in the war with the Tamil Tigers. A Sri Lankan army commander told Nordstrom:

> It is crazy, it's completely crazy. I can't control my troops. It is awful up there. One of the soldiers (government, largely Sinhalese) is shot by a guerrilla (Tamil), or they run over a land mine, or a bomb explodes, and they go nuts. It's been building up and building up, and they just go wild. The guerrillas have long since melted away, and the soldiers turn their fury on the first available target. Of course, the only people around are civilians. They open fire on everyone, they destroy everything in sight, they rape, and torture people they catch on the street or in their homes, they lob bombs into homes and schools, markets and city streets. I've tried to stop them; I try to control the situation. I can't. None of us commanders can – though god knows some don't try. The troops just take off like this and there's no stopping them. We can't discipline them. We can't prosecute them. We can't dismiss them. We'd have no army left if we did. The situation up north is completely out of control, and there isn't a damn thing we can do about it.

One of the purposes of war is to wreak destruction on the enemy. The napalm bombing of Vietnam in the Vietnam War was devastating and the humiliation and torture committed in Abu Ghraib prison in Iraq were anything but humanitarian acts. The aim of the increasingly sophisticated warfare technology now used by the USA and its allies in the wars in Iraq and Afghanistan is to identify its targets more accurately in order to minimize collateral damage and, above all, to minimize its own casualties. 'This humanitarian concern means that soldiers need no longer go to war expecting to die but only to kill' (Asad 2007: 35).

In short, war and terrorism both kill civilians and combatants. The difference between war killing and terrorism is that, under international law, war is legally and morally sanctioned while acts of terrorism are not. Soldiers too are trained to kill and to demonize the enemy through military training and they also go to war primarily to kill. War and terrorism are constituted according to different logical criteria, one taking its primary sense from the question of legality and the other from feelings of vulnerability and fear, and they are not, therefore, mutually exclusive. It is not true to say that terrorism is singularly evil because it kills civilians and inserts a fear in the daily rhythm of life which imposes 'the endless coerciveness of precaution' because war, whether just or unjust, does that too (ibid).

War killing and murder

To understand the nature of the act which, as noted earlier, invariably involves deaths of non-combatant civilians, one has to ask whether the resulting deaths are truly homicidal killings or are actually casualties of war. Homicide is the killing of another person, either intentionally or unintentionally. In human societies, the act of homicide is universally regarded as a crime and in many cases accorded capital punishment. The logic behind capital punishment is to dispose of individuals who have committed an act which is regarded by members of the group to be harmful or threatening to them and to their society. War, on the on the other hand, is organized lethal violence between spatially different groups in which the deaths of other persons are envisioned in advance. In war, therefore, the killing of members of the other group regarded as the enemy is viewed as a justified or justifiable act and consequently is not regarded as murder deserving capital punishment (Otterbein 1986; Kelly 2000).

To determine whether a suicide attack and the resulting deaths of non-combatants constitute murderous killing or casualties of war requires a delineation of the boundaries between war and murder. While participants in some forms of altercations and disputes may employ deadly weapons to kill others, war is the only activity which entails lethal violence that is collectively organized and carried out. Another key – and possibly the unique – feature of war is that 'the deaths of other persons are envisioned in advance and this envisioning is encoded in the purposeful act of taking up lethal weapons' (Kelly 2000: 4).

As organized violence, war requires advance planning and involves a complex division of labour based on the specialization of different types of activities that contribute to warfare. Rational calculations, planning and organization make war instrumentally different from other related forms of violence such as brawls and riots which derive their nature from their affective spontaneity. War also differs from murder and other related forms of violence in that the use of deadly weapons and force is seen as entirely legitimate by the collectivity that resorts to war (Otterbein 1986: 1–47; Kelly 2000: 1–10, Walzer 2004; Grimland, Apter and Kerkof 2006).

Moral appropriateness is integral to the act of making war. Group members are explicitly recruited to the project of causing the deaths of other persons on the grounds that it is legitimate and proper to do so (O'Donovan 2003; Walzer 2004). Because war is always collectively sanctioned, participation in war is regarded as an act of national pride and highly laudable. Men and women become potential or actual 'killers' and those who die in war are recognized as national heroes and martyrs. Such characterizations of the fallen in war contrast sharply with murder which is negatively valued by the social collectivity that constitutes the killer's reference group and is consequently regarded as an illegitimate and criminal act warranting retribution, not social recognition. Murder is culturally disapproved of, stigmatizing rather than prestigious, and falls somewhere along an evaluative scale that extends from regrettable to heinous.

Killing in war and murder are similar in several ways. Both involve deadly violence and bring grief to the affected parties. The punishment for murder and the punishment enacted on the enemy in war killing are regarded as morally appropriate, justified and legitimate actions constituting fulfilment of civic duty. But there is one very critical difference between punishment for murder and punishment of the enemy in war. The death penalty, an almost universal punishment norm for murder, is only applicable to a specific individual, the murderer, whose death expunges the wrong doer from society. War does not excise killers from society but instead targets other individuals who are innocent of direct responsibility for prior killing. In war, the killing of any member of the enemy group is considered legitimate.

War is grounded in the application of the principle of social substitutability and is thus governed by a distinctive logic that is entirely foreign to murder. In war, the killing of an individual is perceived as an injury to his or her group because the logic of war is predicated on group responsibility, thus making any member of the killer's collectivity a legitimate target for retaliation. In war, the anger generated by a prior killing or prior action is redirected to an entirely different individual sufficiently peripheral to be unsuspecting. The principle that one group member is substitutable for another in the context of war underwrites the interrelated concepts of injury to the group, group responsibility for the infliction of injury, and group liability with respect to retribution. War is thus cognitively, conceptually and behaviourally conducted between groups. Murder, on the other hand, is always conceptualized as deadly violence between individual members of the same collectivity (Kelly 2000: 5).

The universal consequence for murder is capital punishment (and now life imprisonment in some countries) which is socially sanctioned and morally justified by the perpetrators' community. It is also carried out after a socially sanctioned and organized process of adjudication by especially appointed members of the community. It can be concluded from the above that there are remarkable similarities between killing in war and murder and one crucial difference (Kelly 2000; Otterbein 1986): in war, killing is directed against any member of the offending party but in murder the action must be directed only against the actual offender.

So, are the casualties from suicide bombing attacks murders or war killing? The preceding discussion and observations would suggest that sociologically, suicide bombing attacks can be classified as a weapon of war and the resulting deaths as war casualties. The groups involved in organizing and sponsoring suicide attacks in the modern world enjoy varying levels of support from their collectivity (N. Hassan 2001; Atran 2003; Bloom 2005; Oliver and Steinberg 2005; Grimland, Apter and Kerkof 2006). They are engaged in conflict over the occupation of their homeland by a foreign army, as a result of which they feel socially and economically dispossessed and humiliated; the occupation of the homeland is seen as sacrilege and as a mortal threat to their political community and its sacred values and way of life (Atran 2006; Ginges *et al.* 2007). Like war, the suicide bombing attack is carefully planned and its execution envisions in advance the deaths of other persons (Pape 2005; Gambetta 2005; Townsend 2007). And like fallen soldiers in war, suicide bombers are regarded by their groups as martyred heroes who have sacrificed their lives for the nation (N. Hassan 2001; Abdel-Khalek 2004; Oliver and Steinberg 2005; Hafez 2007a).

Good death bad death

Why are some types of deaths received with moral revulsion while others are accepted as normal or heroic? Suicide bombings universally evoke a multiplicity of emotions ranging from disbelief to horror, anger, revulsion and condemnation. This is most likely the reason why characterization of these acts as immoral, murderous killings by scholars like Michael Walzer are widely accepted and endorsed by the media, politicians and the general public. Are such emotional and moral reactions to the deaths of innocent people 'natural' human responses? If this is so, then why do equally horrifying deaths caused by natural disasters such as fires, earthquakes, and accidents (air and car crashes) or death caused by national armies fighting wars and terrorism evoke sadness but generally no moral revulsion? Human attitudes towards death – the physical end of the body – cover a wide spectrum of emotions including, for example, sadness, pain, anger, denial, approval and moral revulsion.

According to liberal doctrine, one of the fundamental conditions for the foundation of political community is the monopolistic control of violence by the state. This presupposes that the morally autonomous individual's natural right to violent self-defence is yielded to the state, making the state sole protector of life and liberty. In others words, for a viable society to exist, individuals must be disempowered from killing or murdering others and themselves. The society then empowers certain specific institutions to cause the death of others at home and abroad, making these institutions death brokers and managers of the trajectories of death and dying in society. As mentioned earlier, the right to kill is the right to behave in violent ways against both citizens who break the original covenant and the uncivilized 'others' who pose a threat to the existence of the political community and the maintenance of social order, as their killing provides security (Tuck 1999; Elias 1985). This is the main justification for wars as well as judicial killing in modern societies.

Death brokering refers to the activities of authorities which render death normatively and culturally appropriate. In human societies, medical and religious institutions perform the primary death brokering functions. They control the death and dying process through their expertise by managing how people die and when. Medicine provides curative and therapeutic knowledge and a monopoly over determining the cause of death thus legitimizing its authority over how and when death might occur. Religion invokes the authority of the divine covenants pertaining to 'good' (religiously sanctioned) death. These two institutions are central in negotiating meanings and the cultural appropriateness of death and dying between the individual and society.

Good death invariably involves the management of the dying process through symptom alleviation as well as attention to the religious, social and cultural needs of the dying and their loved ones in order to achieve the normative goal of impending death (Timmermans 2005; Kubler-Ross 1969). A good death, in other words, involves 'disempowering' the dying person in respect of all decisions over death and the dying process. 'Bad' death, by the same logic, is when these characteristics are absent and the individual has control over how and when to die or kill. For example, a death that is negotiated through therapeutic procedures administered by authorised medical personnel is a culturally appropriate death and thus a 'good' death, although the dying person has more or less no power over the dying process. I call this 'disempowered death'. Death that occurs under circumstances in which the dying person has some control over the dying process and the timing of death, a kind of 'empowered death', is socially and culturally inappropriate death or 'bad' death. Good death is 'normal' and evokes appropriate human emotional responses, mostly of grief and sadness. Bad death, on the other hand, is 'abnormal' and therefore stigmatized and evokes a variety of emotional responses including disbelief, anger and revulsion. The reason why suicidal bombing is stigmatized and evokes the type of emotional responses which lie behind its characterization as homicidal and immoral killing is that it combines two types of stigmatized or 'bad' deaths: suicide and murder.

Concluding remarks

Is suicide bombing homicidal killing or a weapon of war? In light of the above discussion, we can say that suicide bombing is not suicide. There appears to be a consensus among scholars that suicide bombing is a different order of behaviour from suicide. Universally, suicide carries a stigma whereas suicide bombings, like war, carry strong approval of the reference group.

What about the difference between war killing and suicide bombing? In political theory, war is legally sanctioned, organized violence which confers legitimacy on the ensuing killing. But the killing perpetrated by suicide bombers is regarded as illegal because of its peculiar evil of targeting innocent civilians and, worse, because it inserts fear and insecurity into everyday life, undermining social order and subjecting society to the 'endless coerciveness of precaution'. It is also regarded as illegal because, unlike those involved in war, militants carrying out terrorism against civilians are not deemed to have reached the last resort and, therefore, are not coerced into action. I have argued that civilians die in war as well as in suicide attacks. In fact, state armies are more capable and efficient killing machines than any terrorist organization; war also injects profound insecurities into the private and public spheres; soldiers are taught to hate and kill enemy combatants and civilians too. The fact of killing in war being legally sanctioned is an abstract irrelevance. There are in fact remarkable similarities between war killing and terrorism.

The case studies of Palestine and Sri Lanka provide evidence that the strategy of targeted suicide bombings was the method of last resort in both cases. Commenting on the rationality of terrorist organizations, Martha Crenshaw points out that efficacy is the primary standard by which terrorism is compared with other methods of achieving political goals. Suicide terror is rarely, if ever, the strategy of first choice but tends to follow other strategies deemed less effective through the process of trial and error. 'Organizations arrive at collective judgements about the relative effectiveness of different strategies ... on the basis of observation and experience, as much as on the basis of abstract strategic conceptions derived from ideological assumptions – allowing for social learning' (Crenshaw 1990: 8).

When all legal means of seeking redress are blocked, human beings react with rage and resort to violence. As Hannah Arendt (1969: 63–64) has observed, to resort to violence when confronted with outrageous events or conditions is enormously tempting because of its inherent immediacy and swiftness in setting the scales of justice right again. What drives suicide bombings in Palestine, Sri Lanka and elsewhere are unbearable sufferings and a desire to reach out to immortality for the sake of the political community. As in the case of fallen soldiers, death constitutes a triumph and a victory. In this respect, the genealogy of the act is profoundly modern and 'this worldly', not 'other worldly'.

The claim of liberal democracies that they have the right to defend themselves with nuclear weapons, which appears to be accepted by the international community, is in effect an affirmation that suicidal war can be legitimate. In this way, the suicide bomber belongs in an important sense to a modern Western tradition of armed conflict for the defence of a free political community. In order to save the nation (or to found its state) by confronting a dangerous enemy, it may be necessary to act without being bound by ordinary moral constraints. Or, as Walzer puts it, 'A morally strong leader is someone who understands why it is wrong to kill the innocent and refuses to do so, refuses again and again, until the heavens are about to fall. And then he becomes a moral criminal who knows that he can't do what he has to do – and finally does' (Walzer 2004: 45). By this reasoning, can the killing of innocents by taking one's own life be the final gesture of a morally strong leader? (Asad 2007: 63)

With regard to war killing and murder, it is argued that suicide bombing attacks are an act and a weapon of war because of the principle of substitutability which characterizes war killing. However, under the International Laws of War, the attacks could most likely be classified as 'war crimes'. Article 147 of the Fourth Geneva Convention defines war crimes as: 'Wilful killing, torture or inhuman treatment, including. ... wilfully causing great suffering or serious injuries to body or health, unlawful deportation or transfer or unlawful confinement of a protected person, compelling a protected person to serve in the forces of hostile powers, or wilfully depriving a protected person of the rights of fair and regular trial. ... taking of hostages and extensive destruction and appropriation of property, not justified by military necessity and carried out unlawfully and wantonly'. But this, of course, would apply not only to the groups organizing and sponsoring suicide bombing but also to the actions of the occupying armies and their military and political leaders.

Finally, death is nature's assertion of mastery over culture. In nature, death and dying are totally amoral events meaning no more than the physical end of a biological organism. But in human cultures, death is embedded with symbols and meanings and classified as *good* and *bad* largely on the basis of the role of socially sanctioned death brokers in its occurrence. In human society, death occurring from acts such as suicide bombing may well be altruistically driven but paradoxically remains stigmatized because it violates one of the fundamental social imperatives for the existence and survival of human society: that individuals are not empowered to take their or someone else's life. This stigma is a natural check that will restrain the diffusion of suicide bombings. From time to time, certain historical conditions may be instrumental in giving rise to phenomena like suicide bombings and may even confer some form of community support but, like other forms of stigmatized deaths, suicide bombings will remain a rare event. Furthermore, it would always provoke the state's strong retaliation against its perpetrators for violating the imperative norms which also act as a strong check on its occurrence, prevalence and diffusion.

5

WHAT HAVE WE LEARNED?

The evidence presented and discussed in the preceding chapters is intended to advance our understanding of the phenomenon of suicide bombing in the modern world by offering some important correctives. The evidence largely discredits explanations that ascribe the cause to the personality of suicide bombers and which assert that suicide bombings are acts of abhorrent violence perpetrated by psychologically impaired, morally deficient, bizarre, sick, crazy, uneducated and impoverished individuals. The public policies which take their cue from such explanations tend to focus on killing, restraining or incarcerating the deranged individuals in order to expunge them from society and not to focus on societal conditions which may have given rise to the phenomenon in the first place.

The genesis of suicide bombings is rooted in intractable asymmetrical conflicts pitching the state against non-state actors over political entitlements, territorial occupation and dispossession. Invariably such conflicts instigate state-sanctioned violence and repressive policies against the weaker non-state party or parties causing widespread outrage and large-scale dislocation of people, many of whom seek refuge in makeshift camps in and outside the 'war zones'. Other contributing factors include the incarceration and humiliation of dissidents, who are often subjected to brutal and dehumanizing treatment in state custody and mutual demonization of the 'other'. Suicide bombing, rarely the strategy of first choice, is selected by terrorist organizations after collective assessments, based on observations and experience, of strategies' relative effectiveness to achieve political goals. It is invariably a weapon of the weak. The following are some of the lessons of this and other recent studies which deserve our attention.

Suicide bombers are not mad

Apart from one demographic attribute – the majority of suicide bombers tend to be young males – recent studies have failed to find a stable set of demographic, psychological, socioeconomic and religious variables that can be causally linked to suicide bombers' personalities or socioeconomic origins. It is argued that labels such as mad, bad, sick, psychologically and morally impaired may be politically and possibly legally expedient, but they do not advance our understanding of the causes of the phenomenon of suicide bombings in a way that can be used to devise preventive public policies. They in fact impede us from discovering its real nature, purpose and causes.

The process of becoming a suicide bomber is gradual and highly selective and acts as a screening mechanism to exclude psychopathological individuals. Candidates who exhibit signs of mental illness are rejected in the interest of group survival. Terrorist groups go to great lengths to recruit members whose behaviour appears to be normal and would not arouse suspicion. Potential members with visible signs of psychopathy would only be a liability for the terrorist group, irrespective of their skills, and could not be relied upon to carry out the assigned mission. On the contrary, such individuals would be likely to botch the operation and sabotage the group by revealing its strategic plans and secrets if captured. Nor would their presence in the group be conducive to enhancing group solidarity. There is now a general consensus among researchers that, with the exception of a few rare cases, there is no apparent connection between violent militant activity and personality disorders. Typically, most suicide bombers are psychologically normal, are deeply integrated into social networks and are emotionally attached to their national communities (Silke 2007a; Sageman 2004; Atran 2003; Pape 2005; N. Hassan 2001; Bloom 2005; Asad 2007; Somasundaram 2010; Aggarwal 2010).

A strategic weapon or tactic

Carefully designed and grounded studies that have significantly contributed to a better understanding of suicide bombings show that they are instrumental and strategic weapons used by well-organized terrorist groups. These groups represent the weaker party in asymmetrical conflicts that are related to the struggle for greater autonomy or liberation of what they regard as their 'homeland'. The deployment of suicide bombings by sponsoring organizations is mainly determined by their cost effectiveness, versatility, lethality and tactical efficiency in reaching well-guarded, high-value targets. Suicide bombings have high symbolic value because the willingness of the perpetrators to die signals high resolve and dedication to their cause. Among sympathetic constituencies, they serve as symbols of a just struggle, galvanize popular support, generate financial backing for the organization and become a source of new recruits for future suicide missions (Pape 2005; Bloom 2005; Hafez 2007b; Atran 2003; Gambetta 2005; Moghadam 2008; Somasundaram 2010). A number of studies have shown that suicide bombings serve the interests of the sponsoring organization in two ways: by coercing an adversary to make concessions and by giving the organization an advantage over its rivals in terms of support from constituencies. From this perspective, understanding the organization's logic is more important than understanding the motivation of individuals in explaining suicide attacks (Pape 2005; Bloom 2005; Hafez 2007b). Contrary to the popular image that suicide terrorism is an outcome of irrational religious fanaticism, suicide bombing attacks are an intensely political phenomenon (Gupta and Mundra 2005; Pape 2005; Bloom 2005; Asad 2007; Somasundaram 2010).

Driven mainly by politics, not religion

The two case studies in this book support findings of other recent studies that the driving force behind suicide bombings is *politics* and not *religion*, though in some cases religion can play a vital role in recruiting and motivating potential future suicide bombers, particularly when secular ideologies fail to bring about desired changes. The case studies show that in both cases the political conflict was over the autonomy or liberation of the 'homeland', and also reveal that suicide bombing was adopted as the weapon of last resort by the sponsoring organizations after long periods of protest, political agitation and other forms of non-violent methods had failed. Sometimes religious differences fuelled the conflict, but it was invariably in the context of a desire for the honourable survival of the political community.

According to Gambetta (2005), between 1981 and 2003, 53 per cent of suicide missions were carried out by secular organizations and 35 per cent by religious (Islamic) organizations. The most suicide attacks in this period were sponsored by the secular Sri Lankan Liberation Tigers of Tamil Eelam. In the case of Iraq, many suicide bombers were radicalized by the Iraq War and not by religion (Hafez 2007b; Regan 2005). This also applied to suicide bombings in Pakistan and Afghanistan. Most of the suicide bombers tend not to be deeply religious. In the case of suicide attackers who carried out suicide missions worldwide between 1981 and 2003, Robert Pape was able to ascertain the ideological background of 83 per cent and found that only 43 per cent were religious (Pape 2005).

The research also indicates significant differences in the profiles of suicide missions and their outcomes. In Sri Lanka and Palestine–Israel, suicide missions were carefully planned and were carried out by terrorist organizations with well-established infrastructures for the recruitment and training of volunteers for future attacks. They had well-developed protocols for planning and executing suicide bombing attacks. Suicide attacks in Iraq, Pakistan and Afghanistan, on the other hand, are not only a recent phenomenon but are also not well planned and executed by the sponsoring organizations. These differences are reflected in the significant variations in the outcomes of suicide missions in terms of their lethality. In Iraq, 9 per cent of all terrorist attacks are suicide attacks compared with 4 per cent in Afghanistan, 5 per cent in Pakistan and 7 per cent in Palestine–Israel. The deaths caused by suicide attacks also vary significantly in these countries. I have argued that these variations clearly can be attributed to the differences in planning and execution of the suicide attacks and the efficiency of the emergency services (R. Hassan 2010).

For the individual, participation in a suicide mission is not about dying and killing alone, but has a broader significance for achieving multiple purposes. These include gaining community approval, political success and the liberation of the homeland as well as personal redemption and honour, and achieving the exalted status of martyr for the survival of the community.

It also signals unwillingness to accept subjugation, allows for revenge for personal and collective humiliation and acts as a symbol of religious or nationalistic convictions; guilt, shame, material and religious rewards, escape from intolerable everyday degradations of life under occupation, boredom, anxiety and defiance. Obviously the configurations of these purposes would vary and would be the result in each case of the specific circumstances of the political conflict that had led to the rise of suicide attacks as a tactic and a weapon (Gambetta 2005; Hafez 2006; Pedahzur 2005; Elster 2005; Pape 2005; Khosrokhavar 2005; El Sarraj 2002; N. Hassan 2001; Atran 2006; Somasundaram 2010; Hassan 2010).

Humiliation aids the sub-culture of suicide bombing

Humiliation, revenge and altruism appear to play key roles at organizational and individual levels in shaping a sub-culture which promotes suicide bombings. Humiliation is a complex and intense, emotional and personal experience that occurs when historically and culturally grounded definitions or perceptions of self-worth, self-respect and dignity are destroyed and revealed as apparently false and illegitimate affectations. Thus, feelings of lowered self-respect are created, which in turn inspire an unwillingness to obey humiliating authority, overt rebellion or simmering resentment. The available evidence suggests that violence, the everyday degradations of occupation, harsh repression, a sense of collective grievances, torture, the violation of culturally grounded codes of honour and shame, massive economic and social dislocations, anxiety and helplessness are powerful means by which to inflict humiliation.

Besides being a painful emotional sensation, humiliation is a potent technique of social control in traditional tribal societies as well as in their modern counterparts. Some political theorists argue that humiliation is one of the principal modern modes of maintaining social order and hierarchy, and go so far as to suggest that it is becoming ever more prevalent (Miller 1993; Saurette 2006). Humiliation has been labelled as the central vice of modern societies. The prominent Israeli political philosopher Avishai Margalit argues that modern institutions play a central role in the production of humiliation. Humiliation arises from the maltreatment of people by society's institutions. A society whose institutions practise this could not be a decent and good society. Margalit describes a decent society as one in which institutions do not humiliate its citizens, and a civilized society as one in which citizens do not humiliate each other (Margalit 1996; Lukes 1997).

Humiliation is different from fear. Fear is an instinctive emotional response to potential danger that can cause physical pain. Humiliation, on the other hand, is an emotional process that seeks to discipline the humiliated party's behaviour by attacking and lowering their own and others' perceptions of whether they deserve respect. In Abu Ghraib prison the techniques – forced nudity, simulated sex with another man in front of a female, being made to bark like a dog and being photographed doing so – were intended not to inflict physical pain but to create total submission and obedience. These and other actions of the US prison guards at Abu Ghraib were disciplinary practices that worked on what it meant to be an honourable, self-respecting subject in Iraqi society. The intensely negative and visceral impact was that of stripping away and revealing as false the most prized self-perceptions and most valued bases of self-respect and dignity. The prison practices were designed to humiliate the subject – that is, make them feel unworthy – and to transform this feeling into a sense that motivated the subject to obey and act in deference to the humiliating authority (Saurette 2006; Hersh 2004; Physicians for Human Rights 2005).

These practices did not humiliate the prisoners alone but were felt and seen as humiliating by all Iraqis (Hersh 2004). This was evident in the reactions that followed the publication of the prisoner abuse photographs. In the months following their release, daily insurgent and suicide bombing attacks in Iraq increased dramatically (see Table 3.1 and Figure 3.2). Similarly, in Iraq, the Palestinian territories, Sri Lanka, Pakistan and Afghanistan, counter-insurgency operations involving random house searches, interrogations, arrests and other violations of human dignity are followed by an increase in suicide attacks.

Sometimes driven by revenge and retaliation

As noted in Chapters 3 and 4, violence and counter-violence permeates all aspects of daily life in war zones associated with suicide bombings. Ordinary routines of daily life that we take for granted become harrowing, onerous and dangerous chores. One's sense of personal security is replaced with a constant fear of unexpected death. Moral bases of social life are severely disrupted. The stripping of human dignity and the constant experience of humiliation appear to become a way of life. The following description of the Palestinian territories by the eminent American psychologist Scott Atran captured the reality of human conditions there in 2004: 'Life in the occupied territories has never been as bad. Northern Gaza is a charred battlefield and almost every West Bank town is ringed by guns, barbed wire, and concrete. The economy is lifeless, except for Ramallah, seat of the Palestinian Authority's dysfunctional ministries – and the NGOs that bring some activity. Palestinians are convinced that Israeli Army checkpoints, where people often wait for hours in shadeless no-man lands or long tunnels, are meant to break their will and drive them from the land. Israelis counter that they nab, on average, at least one suicide bomber a day at the checkpoints and that Palestinians confuse cause – suicide bombing – with effect – extreme vigilance to stop it' (Atran 2004). The middle-class students at Al-Najah University in Nablus, who provide more suicide bombers than any other demographic group in the Palestinian territories, told Scott Atran, 'Martyrs give us dignity to free ourselves' (Atran 2004). Their attitudes underscored the collective sentiments of many Palestinian people.

In human societies, such experiences evoke an intense desire for revenge. Humans appear to have an incredibly strong sense of justice, and a desire for revenge is the darker side to this. Psychologists define revenge and vengeance as 'the infliction of harm in return for perceived injury or insult or as simply getting back at another person' (Cota-McKinley, Woody and Bell 2001: 343). An important element of the desire for vengeance is the surprising willingness of individuals to sacrifice in order to carry out an act of revenge. Revenge has irrational and destructive consequences for the person seeking vengeance as well as for the target. One of them is that the person seeking vengeance is willing to compromise his or her own integrity, social standing and personal safety for the sake of revenge. Why are people willing to pay such high costs, and what ends are served by revenge?

Revenge can fulfil a range of goals, including righting perceived injustices, restoring the self-worth of the vengeful individual and deterring future injustice. It is also a response to the continuous suffering of an aggrieved community. At the heart of the whole process are perceptions of personal harm, unfairness and injustice, and the anger, indignation and hatred associated with the perceived injustice. In other words, the desire for revenge and the willingness to carry out violence are tied to the self-worth of the offended person and to a deterrent role against future injustices. Studies have revealed that some groups are more vengeance-prone than others: men hold more positive attitudes towards vengeance than women, for example, and young people are more prepared to act in a vengeful manner than older individuals (Cota-McKinley, Woody and Bell 2001; Kim and Smith 1993). It is not surprising, then, to find that most suicide bombers are both young and male.

Personal histories of suicide bombers often contain accounts of encounters with the security forces or rival groups that have involved threats, harassment, assaults and even deaths of those near and dear to the bomber. Many studies of suicide bombers reveal that the main motivating force for the suicide bombers seems to be a desire for spectacular revenge (Silke 2003, 2007a; Pape 2005; Bloom 2005; Hafez 2007b; N. Hassan 2001; Pedahzur 2005; Margalit 2003; Berko 2007; Somasundaram 1998, 2008b; El Sarraj 2002; Speckhard and Ahkmedova 2006; Gupta and Mundra 2005; Strenski 2003; Post and Denny 2002). On 4 October 2003, 29-year-old Palestinian lawyer Hanadi Jaradat exploded her suicide belt in the Maxim restaurant in Haifa, killing twenty people and wounding many more. According to her family, her suicide mission was in revenge for the killing of her brother and her fiancé by the Israeli security forces and for all the crimes Israel was perpetrating in the West Bank by killing Palestinians and expropriating their lands (Brym 2007). The main motive of many suicide bombers in Israel is revenge for acts committed by Israelis (Margalit 2003). In the Israeli context, if revenge is the principal goal, the suicide bombers have succeeded in hurting Israel very badly, and not just by killing and injuring many civilians:

> A more far-reaching success is that Israel's leaders, in retaliating, have behaved so harshly, putting three million people under siege, with recurring curfews for unlimited periods of time, all in front of the world press and television, with the result that Israel may now be the most hated country in the world, which is hugely damaging to Israel, since the difference between being hated and losing legitimacy is dangerously narrow. Throughout the world, moreover, the suicide bombings have more often been taken as a sign of the desperation of the Palestinians than as acts of terror.
>
> *(Margalit 2003: 8)*

Similar observations have been made in the context of other sites of suicide bombings in the modern world (Strenski 2003; Asad 2007; Hafez 2007b). The motivations of vengeful actions have a strong altruistic component which manifests itself in the act of self-sacrifice for the sake of one's family, community or ideology. As has been noted in this and other studies of suicide bombers, in carrying out their actions they are aware that their vengeful action in the form of self-sacrifice will be recognized and celebrated by the community to which they belong. Vengeance through suicide bombing has an additional value: that of making oneself the victim of one's own act, thereby putting one's tormentors to moral shame. The idea of suicide bombing, unlike that of an ordinary attack, is, perversely, a moral idea in which the killers, in acting out the drama of being the ultimate victim, claim for their cause the moral high ground (Margalit 2003; see also Strenski 2003; Asad 2007).

In the face of apparent injustice and the absence of external redress, a personal motivation for revenge is very common and a wretchedly stable aspect of human nature. It is also true that this motivation will not be taken up by many of the aggrieved. But for some individuals, and in some circumstances, this motivation will provoke violence. There is nothing strange and bizarre about this. The desire for violent revenge and the willingness to act on it are expected human reactions to certain situations (Silke 2003). Hannah Arendt takes an even stronger stance in her discussion of the human response to perceived injustices when legal means of seeking redress are blocked. She argues that under such conditions human beings react with rage and resort to the violence of revenge.

> Rage is by no means an automatic reaction to misery as such ... Only where there is reason to suspect that conditions could be changed and are not does the rage arise. Only when our sense of justice is offended do we react with rage, and this reaction by no means necessarily reflects personal injury ... To resort to violence when confronted with outrageous events or conditions is enormously tempting because of its inherent immediacy and swiftness ... The point is that under certain circumstances – acting without argument or speech and without counting the consequences – is the only way to set the scales of justice right again ... In this sense, rage and the violence that sometimes – not always – goes with it belong to the 'natural' human

emotions, and to cure man of them would mean nothing less than to dehumanise or emasculate him.

(Arendt 1969: 63–64)

Altruistically driven action

While suicide is an integral part of suicide bombing, its meaning and nature in this context are strikingly different from ordinary suicide. One of the main differences between the two acts is that in suicide bombing the primary intention of the act is to kill others who have no prior relationship with the suicide bomber, whereas the primary characteristic of suicide is the absence of murderous intent. In Durkheim's conceptual map (1951), suicide bombing would fall into the rare category of altruistic suicidal actions. These are distinct from other types of suicidal actions caused by personal catastrophes, hopelessness and psychopathologies which lead people to believe that life is not worth living. Altruistic suicides, on the other hand, involve valuing one's life as less worthy than the group's honour, religion, or some other collective interest. In its very essence, altruism is a costly action which benefits others. Altruism is a fundamental condition explaining human co-operation for the organization of society and its cohesiveness (Fehr and Fischbacher 2003).

Using insights from rational choice theory, economists link suicide bombings to altruism as a form of intergenerational investment. Suicide bombing is stipulated as an extreme form of saving. The agent gives up any current consumption for the sake of enhancing the probability of his/her descendants enjoying the benefits of future public good. A recent study of Hezbollah suicide bombers shows that incidents of suicide attacks increase with current income and with the degree of altruism towards the next generation. The data also demonstrate that Hezbollah suicide bombers come from above-averagely wealthy families, and have an above-average level of education. These two factors should have opposing effects: while the higher-class origin of the bombers is consistent with the model, the higher education level of bombers and their higher accumulated human capital normally should act as deterrents to suicide bombing, but in this case they do not, suggesting that an individual's education level probably has an independent effect on his or her willingness to engage in suicide missions. Education affects deeply one's view of the world, enhancing one's sensitivity to the future, thus making educated people more sensitive to the fate of future generations (Azam 2005; Sayre 2009).

Altruism is also not antithetical to aggression. In war, soldiers perform altruistic actions by risking their lives for their comrades and country, also killing the enemy. Similarly, as noted in the opening chapter, the actions of historical personas like the Roman soldier statesman Cato, the martyr founder of the Shia sect of Islam, Husayn ibn Ali, at Kerbala in 680, the martyrs of Cordoba, Jewish Sicarii and Jesus Christ in his crucifixion death were altruistic suicidal missions. In more recent history, the actions of kamikaze pilots in World War II and the heroic deeds of the Victoria Cross awardees in the British Commonwealth are examples of military sacrifice. Altruism can also be socially constructed in communities which have endured massive social and economic dislocations as a result of long, violent and painful conflict with a more powerful enemy. Under such conditions, people react to perceived inferiority and the failure of other efforts by valuing and supporting ideals of self-sacrifice such as suicide bombing. Religiously and nationalistically coded attitudes towards the acceptance of death stemming from long periods of collective suffering, humiliation and powerlessness enable political organizations to give people suicide bombings as an outlet for their feelings of desperation, deprivation, hostility and injustice.

Paradoxically, actions such as suicide bombings invariably provoke a brutal response from the state authorities because, by injecting fear and mayhem into the ordinary rhythms of daily life, they threaten and undermine the state's authority in providing security of life and property and in maintaining social order. And under such conditions, the state can legitimately impose *altruistic punishments* to deter future violation of social norms threatening security and social order (Fehr and Gachter 2002). These include punishments meted out to the perpetrators and their supporters. The state-sanctioned military actions against the Palestinians, Sri Lankan Tamil Tigers, Iraqi insurgents and the Taliban in Pakistan and Afghanistan are examples of these punishments. But recent experimental studies by Fehr and others have shown that altruistic punishments are only effective when they do not violate the norms of *fairness*. Punishments and sanctions seen as unfair, hostile, selfish and vindictive by targeted groups tend to have detrimental effects and, instead of promoting compliance, they reinforce recipients' resolve to resort to non-compliance (Fehr and Rockenbach 2003; Fehr and Gachter 2002).

Counter-insurgency operations are aimed at increasing the cost of non-compliance to the insurgents. They invariably involve eliminating leaders and supporters who plan suicide bombings and destroying insurgents' capacity to mount future attacks, as well as the imposition of restrictions on mobility, security checks and other violations of civil liberties. But there is mounting evidence that such harsh measures actually reinforce radical opposition and even intensify it. This is what is now happening in Pakistan, Afghanistan and the Palestinian territories. It has also been the case in Sri Lanka and Iraq and other conflict sites. The most likely explanation of this is the one suggested by the studies of *altruistic punishments* referred to above, that when collective sanctions and punishments are seen by the targeted populations to be violating the norms of *fairness*, they become counter-productive. Instead of increasing the cost of insurgency, they escalate the cost of counter-insurgency operations by increasing non-compliance and hardening resistance, which then creates a cycle of harsher and more dangerous counter-insurgency operations followed by more non-compliance and violent resistance.

The empirical validation of this is provided by a study of Hamas and Palestinian Jihad leaders. They were asked through in-depth interviews whether five years (2000–05) of harsh Israeli repression involving targeted assassination of leaders, numerous arrests, raids on bomb-making facilities, demolition of houses belonging to family members of suicide bombers and so on, had affected their organization's ability to conduct suicide bombing operations. 33 per cent said that it had increased and 42 per cent said it had not affected the organization's ability, and 100 per cent said they would never be willing to recognize the legitimacy of the state of Israel. The Israeli policy had increased their resolve to conduct violent resistance (Brym 2007: 44–45; Brym and Araj 2006). Similar trends are emerging among the Pakistani and Afghan Taliban leaders (Rashid 2008a; Atran 2010).

Studies of social movements indicate that while state repression may reduce overt expressions of protests, it strengthens protest movements by successfully forging and encouraging alliances and cross-cutting coalitions among disparate resistance actors and groups, paving the way for greater solidarity and co-operation between them in future. These studies also reveal the continuing growth of resistance movements even during the low points in their developmental cycle. More specifically, they suggest a *repression paradox*: state repression depresses collective action of a conventional and confrontational type but fails to prevent unobtrusive mobilizations which can signal a solidarity that becomes a powerful resource when opportunities arise. In other words, organizations and groups use adaptive strategies to cope with increasing coercion, but in the following stages they emerge as stronger and more cohesive to mount greater resistance against state repression (Chang 2008; Weiss 2006; Tarrow 1998; Khawaja 1994). The developmental trajectories of some of the powerful terrorist insurgent organizations, including Hezbollah, Hamas, Liberation Tigers of Tamil Eelam, Al-Qaeda in Iraq, Al Qaeda, Tehrik-i-Taliban Pakistan, Jaish-e-Muhammad and Lashkar-e-Toiba, offer empirical validation of this phenomenon.

Countering suicide terrorism

The contention of this study is that the causes of suicide bombings lie not in individual psychopathology but in the broader human condition. Suicide terrorism emerges under certain societal conditions, and understanding and knowledge of these conditions is vital for developing appropriate public policies and responses to protect the public from it. Profiling potential suicide bombers and conducting state sanctioned repression do not appear to be effective public policies. Profiling is expensive, ineffective and alienating. State-sanctioned repression is a boomerang: instead of preventing it, repression escalates suicide terrorism, and where repression appears to have succeeded in its aim, the human and economic costs have created unprecedented humanitarian crises. Any success, therefore, may be a temporary reprieve rather than a lasting relief. Amongst the most fertile environments for nurturing the sub-culture of suicide bombings are the refugee camps in the Palestinian territories, Sri Lanka, Pakistan and Afghanistan; and the dehumanizing treatment of prisoners in these and other countries also encourages its growth. Strategies for eliminating or at least addressing the problems of economic deprivation, humiliation and related collective grievances in concrete and effective ways would have a significant and, in many cases, immediate impact on alleviating the conditions that nurture the sub-cultures of suicide bombings.

In the final analysis, suicide bombings are carried out by community-based organizations. Strategies aimed at findings ways to induce communities to abandon such support may isolate terrorist organizations and curtail their activities. But ultimately, strategies addressing and lessening the grievances and humiliations of populations that give rise to suicide bombing attacks are required for their elimination. Support for suicide bombing attacks is unlikely to diminish without tangible progress in achieving at least some of the fundamental goals that suicide bombers and those sponsoring and supporting them share.

Death is nature's assertion of mastery over culture. In nature, death and dying are totally amoral events, meaning no more than the physical end of a biological organism. But in human cultures, death is embedded with symbols and meanings and classified as *good* and *bad*, largely on the basis of the role of socially sanctioned death brokers in its occurrence. As argued in Chapter 4, death in human society occurring from acts such as suicide bombing may well be altruistically driven but paradoxically remains stigmatized because it violates one of the fundamental social imperatives for the existence and survival of human society: that individuals are not empowered to take their or someone else's life. This stigma, I have argued, is a natural check that will restrain the diffusion of suicide bombings. From time to time, certain historical conditions may be instrumental in giving rise to phenomena such as suicide bombings, and may even confer some form of community support, but, like other forms of stigmatized deaths, suicide bombings will remain a rare event. Furthermore, it will always provoke the state's strong retaliation against its perpetrators for their violation of the imperative norms which also act as a strong check on its occurrence, prevalence and diffusion.

APPENDIX

TABLE A Suicide Bombing Attacks 2007–2008: New cases from GTD

Country	*Incidents*	*Minimum killed*	*Maximum killed*
Aghanistan	80	557	637
Algeria	10	154	164
China	1	3	4
France	3	0	3
Georgia	1	0	1
UK	1	0	1
Greece	1	0	1
India	2	3	5
Iran	2	4	6
Iraq	196	2,901	3,097
Israel	2	12	14
Kenya	1	3	4
Lebanon	2	18	20
Morocco	5	3	8
Pakistan	68	1,053	1,121
Philippines	1	1	2
Russia	3	14	17

TABLE A Cont'd

Country	*Incidents*	*Minimum killed*	*Maximum killed*
Somalia	5	20	25
Sri Lanka	9	57	66
Syria	1	18	19
Turkey	1	1	2
Yemen	2	25	27
Total	**397**	**4,847**	**5,244**

References

The National Consortium for the Study of Terrorism and Responses to Terrorism (START), 2010; Global Terrorism Database (GTD), accessed online 16 August 2010: http://www.start.umd.edu/gtd/search/Results.aspx?start_yearonly=&end_yearonly=&start_year=2007&start_month=1&start_day=1&end_year=2008&end_month=12&end_day=31&asmSelect0=&asmSelect1=&sAttack=1&dtp2=some&success=yes&casualties_type=b&casualties_max=

BIBLIOGRAPHY

Abdel-Khalek, Ahmad M. (2004) 'Neither altruistic suicide, nor terrorism by martyrdom: A Muslim perspective,' *Archives of Suicide Research*, 8(1): 99–113.

Aggarwal, N.K. (2010) 'How are suicide bombers analysed in mental health discourse? A critical anthropological reading', *Asian Journal of Social Science*, 38:347–91.

Ahmed, Hisham H. (2005) 'Palestinian resistance and "suicide bombing": Causes and consequences', in T. Bjorgo (ed.), *Root Causes of Terrorism: Myths, Reality and Ways Forward*, London: Routledge, pp. 87–102.

Ahmed, M. (1992) 'Islam and the state: The case of Pakistan', in M. Moen and L. Gustafson (eds), *Religious Challenge to the State*, Philadelphia: Temple University Press, pp. 239–67.

Amnesty International (1986) *Sri Lanka Disappearances*, AI Index: ASA 37/08/86, London.

—— (2002) *Without Distinction: Attacks by Palestinian Armed Groups*, New York: Amnesty International.

Araj, Bader (2008) 'Harsh state repression as a cause of suicide bombings: The case of the Palestinian–Israeli conflict', *Studies in Conflict and Terrorism*, 31(4):284–303.

Arendt, Hannah (1969) *On Violence*, London: Allen Lane.

Argo, Nicole (2003) 'The banality of evil, understanding today's human bombs', unpublished policy paper, Preventive Defence Project, Stanford University.

—— (2004) 'Understanding and defusing human bombs: The Palestinian case and the pursuit of a martyrdom complex', Working Paper, Preventive Defence Project, Stanford University.

ARTIS Report: (2009) *'Theoretical Frames on pathways to Violent Radicalization: Understanding the Evolution of Ideas and behaviour, How They Interact and How They Descibe Pathways to Violence in Marginalized Diaspora', report to the Office of Naval Research, August 2009:* http://www.artisresearch.com/articles/ARTIS_Theoretical_Frames_August_2009.pdf.

Asad, Talal (2007) *On Suicide Bombing*, New York: Columbia University Press.

Atran, Scott (2003) 'Genesis of suicide terrorism', *Science*, 299(5612):1534–39.

—— (2004) 'Let liberty transform Palestine, too', *The Christian Science Monitor*, 24 October. www.csmoitor.com/2004/1027/p09s01-coop.html.

—— (2006) 'The moral logic and growth of suicide terrorism', *Washington Quarterly*, 29(2):127–47.

—— (2010) 'A question of honour: Why the Taliban fight and what to do about it' *Asian Journal of Social Science*, 38:341–61.

Atran, S. (2010) '*Pathways to and from Violent Extremism: The Case for Science Based Field Research*' Statement Before the [US] Senate Armed Services Subcommittee on Emerging Threats & Capabilities, March 10, 2010, Washington DC.

Azam, J. (2005) 'Suicide-bombing as intergenerational investment', *Public Choice*, 122:177–98.

Barraclough, B. and Harris, C. (2002) 'Suicide preceded by murder: The epidemiology of homicide-suicide in England and Wales', *Psychological Medicine*, 32:577–84.

Barzilai, Anat (2001) 'Stereotypes of Muslims in Israeli press', unpublished paper, Department of Sociology, University of California: Los Angeles.

Battin, M. (2004) 'The effects of self sacrifice: What is wrong with suicide bombings?' Archives of Suicide Research, 8(1):38–42.

Berko, Anat (2007) *The Path to Paradise: The Inner World of Suicide Bombers and their Dispatchers*, London: Praeger Security International.

Berman, Eli and Laitin, David D. (2005) 'Hard targets: Theory and evidence on suicide arracks', Working Paper 11740, National Bureau of Economic Research, Cambridge, MA. www.nber.org/papers/w11740.

Bloom, Mia (2004) 'Palestinian suicide bombing: Public support, market share, and outbidding', *Political Science Quarterly*, 119(1):39–59.

—— (2005) *Dying to Kill: The Allure of Suicide Terror*, New York: Columbia University Press.

Bonner, Raymond (2006) 'Scholar revises terrorism research plan', *New York Times*, 14 September.

Bourke, Joanna (1999) *An Intimate History of Killing: Face-to-Face Killing in Twentieth-Century Warfare*, New York: Basic Books.

Brym, Robert J. (2007) 'Six lessons of suicide bombers', *Contexts*, 6(4):40–45.

Brym, Robert J. and Araj, Bader (2006) 'Suicide bombing as strategy and interaction: The case of the Second Intifada', *Social Forces*, 84(4):1965–82.

—— (2008) 'Palestinian suicide bombing revisited: A critique of the outbidding thesis', *Political Science Quarterly*, 123(3):483–500.

Butler, Linda (2002) 'Suicide bombers: Dignity, despair, and the need for hope', Journal of Palestine *Studies*, 31(4):71–76.

Chang, P. (2008) 'Unintended consequences of repression: Alliance formation in South Korea's democracy movement (1970–79), *Social Forces*, 87(2):652–77.

Christys, Ann (2002) *Christians in al-Andalus (711–1000)*, Richmond: Curzon Press.

Colbert, Edward P. (1962) *The Martyrs of Cordoba (850–859): A Study of Sources*, Washington, DC: Catholic University of America Press.

Coope, Jessica A. (1995) *The Martyrs of Cordoba: Community and Family Conflict in an Age of Mass Conversion*, Lincoln, NE: University of Nebraska Press.

Cordesman, A. (2005) Iraq's Evolving Insurgency, Washington, DC: Centre for Strategic and International Studies.

Cota-McKinley, A., Woody, W. and Bell, P. (2001) 'Vengeance: Effects of gender, age and religious background', *Aggressive Behaviour*, 27:343–50.

Crenshaw, Martha (1990) 'The logic of terrorism: Terrorist behaviour as product of strategic choice', in W. Reich (ed.), *Origins of Terrorism: Psychologies, Ideologies, Theologies, States of Mind*, New York: Cambridge University Press.

—— (2002) '"Suicide terrorism" in comparative perspective', in *Countering Suicide Terrorism*, Herzliya, Israel: International Policy Institute for Counter Terrorism.

—— (2007) 'Explaining suicide terrorism: A review essay', *Security Studies*, 16(1):133–62.

Curiel, J. (2000).'The mind of suicide bomber', *San Francisco Chronicle*, October 22

Dabbagh, Nadia Taysir (2005) *Suicide in Palestine: Narratives of Despair*, Northampton, MA: Olive Branch Press.

Daniel, Norman (1979) *The Arabs and Medieval Europe*, London: Longman.

Davis, J.M. (2003) *Martyrs: Innocence, Vengeance, and Despair in the Middle East*, New York: Palgrave.

deMause, L. (2002) 'The childhood origins of terrorism', *Journal of Psychohistory*, 29(4):340–48.

Doney, A. (1998) 'The Psychological after-effects of torture: A survey of Sri Lankan sacrifice' in D.J. Somasudaram ed. Scarred Minds: The Psychological Impact of War on Sri Lankan Tamils, New Delhi: Sage, pp. 256–87.

Durkheim, Emile (1951) *Suicide: A Study in Sociology*, London: Routledge & Kegan Paul.

Edwards, Verity and Stewart, Cameron (2006) 'Professor warned off terrorist trip', *Australian*, 12 September.

El Sarraj, Eyad (2002) 'Suicide bombers: Dignity, despair, and the need of hope', *Journal of Palestine Studies*, 31(4):71–76.

Elias, N. (1985) *The Loneliness of Dying*, Oxford: Basil Blackwell.

Elster, Jon (2005) 'Motivations and beliefs in suicide bombings', in D. Gambetta (ed.), *Making Sense of Suicide Missions*, Oxford: Oxford University Press, pp. 233–58.

Fehr, E. and Fischbacher, U. (2003) 'The nature of human altruism', *Nature*, 425:785–89.

Fehr, E. and Gachter, S. (2002) 'Altruistic punishment in humans', *Nature*, 415:137–40.

Fehr, Ernest and Rockenbach, Bettina (2003) 'Detrimental effects of sanctions on human altruism', *Nature*, 422:137–40.

Gambetta, Diego (ed.) (2005) *Making Sense of Suicide Missions*, Oxford: Oxford University Press.

Ganor, Boaz (2002) 'Suicide attacks in Israel', in *Countering Suicide Terrorism*, Herzliya, Israel: International Policy Institute for Counter Terrorism, pp. 140–54.

Gilligan, J. (2000) *Violence: Reflections on Our Deadliest Epidemic*, London: Jessica Kingsley.

Ginges, J., Atran, S., Medin, S. and Shikaki, K. (2007) 'Sacred bounds on rational resolution of violent political conflict', *Proceedings of the National Academy of Science of the USA*, 104(18):7357–60.

Goldenberg, S. (2002) 'The men behind the suicide bombers: Every death is the product of a well-oiled machine' *Guardian*, 12 June.

Grimland, M., Apter, A. and Kerkhof, A. (2006) 'The phenomenon of suicide bombings: A review of psychological and non-psychological factors', *Crisis: The Journal of Crisis Intervention and Suicide Prevention*, 27(3):107–18.

Gunaratna, R. (2000) 'The LTTE and suicide terrorism', *Frontline*, 17:3 February.

—— (2002) *Inside Al Qaeda*, London: Hurst.

Gupta, D.K. and Mundra, K. (2005) 'Suicide bombing as a strategic weapon: Empirical investigation of Hamas and Islamic Jihad', *Terrorism and Political Violence*, 17(4):573–98.

Hafez, Mohammad M. (2006) *Manufacturing Human Bombs: The Making of Palestinian Suicide Bombers*, Washington, DC: United States Institute of Peace Press.

—— (2007a) 'Martyrdom mythology in Iraq: How jihadists frame suicide terrorism in videos and biographies', *Terrorism and Political Violence*, 19(1): 95–115.

—— (2007b) *Suicide Bombers in Iraq: The Strategy and Ideology of Martyrdom*, Washington, DC: United States Institute of Peace Press.

Hassan, Nasra (2001) 'An arsenal of believers: Talking to the human bombs', *New Yorker*, 19 November:36–41.

Hassan, Riaz (1985) 'Islamization: An analysis of religious, political and social change in Pakistan', *Middle Eastern Studies*, 21(3):263–84.

—— (1995) *Suicide Explained: The Australian Experience*, Melbourne: Melbourne University Press.

—— (2001) 'Is suicide a disease?', *Medical Journal of Australia*, 19(10):554–55.

—— (2007) 'Some observations on the Sunni–Shia divide and its global implications', paper presented at the International Institute for Counter Terrorism's 2007 International Conference, Herzliya, Israel.

—— (2008) *Inside Muslim Minds*, Melbourne: Melbourne University Publishing.

—— (2009) 'Interrupting a history of tolerance: Anti-Semitism and the Arabs', *Asian Journal of Social Science*, 37(3):453–62.

—— (2010) *Life as a Weapon: The Global Rise of Suicide Bombings*, London and New York: Routledge.

Healy, Guy (2008) 'Support for terror research', *Australian*, 6 August.

Hellmann-Rajanayagam, Dagmar (1994) *The Tamil Tigers: Armed Struggle for Identity*, Stuttgart: Franz Steiner Verlag.

Hersh, Seymour M. (2004) 'Torture at Abu Ghraib', *New Yorker*, 10 May.

—— (2008) 'Preparing the battlefield: Bush administration steps up its secret move against Iran', *New Yorker*, 7 July, www.newyorker.com/reprints/2008/07/07080707fa_fact_hersh?printbale = true (accessed 7 July 2008).

Hill, Peter (2005) 'Kamikaze, 1943–45', in Diego Gambetta (ed.), *Making Sense of Suicide Missions*, Oxford: Oxford University Press.

Hoffman, Bruce and McCormick, Gordon H. (2004) 'Terrorism, signalling, and suicide attack', *Studies in Conflict and Terrorism*, 27(4):243–81.

Holland, T. (2003) *Rubicon: The Triumph and Tragedy of the Roman Republic*, London: Little, Brown.

Hopgood, S. (2005) 'Tamil Tigers, 1987–2002', in Diego Gambetta (ed.), *Making Sense of Suicide Missions*, Oxford: Oxford University Press, pp. 43–76.

Horgan, J. (2003) 'The search for the terrorist personality', in A. Silke (ed.), *Terrorist, Victims and Society: Psychological Perspective on Terrorism and its Consequences*, Chichester: Wiley, pp. 3–27.

Hudson, Rex (1999) *The Sociology and Psychology of Terrorism: Who Becomes a Terrorist and Why?* Washington, DC: Library of Congress.

Israeli, R. (1997) 'Islamikaze and their significance', *Terrorism and Political Violence*, 9(3):96–121.

—— (2003) *Islamikaze: Manifestations of Islamic Martyrology*, London: Frank Cass.

Jayyusi, May (2004) 'Subjectivity and public witness: An analysis of Islamic militancy in Palestine', unpublished paper for the SSRC Beirut Conference on Public Sphere in the Middle East.

Jayyusi, Salma Khadra (ed.) (1992) *The Legacy of Muslim Spain*, Leiden: E.J. Brill.

Jiryes, S. (1973) *The Arab in Israel*, Beirut: Institute for Palestine Studies.

Joiner, T. (2006) *Why People Die by Suicide*, Cambridge, MA: Harvard University Press.

Joshi, Charu Lata (2000) 'Ultimate sacrifice: Faced with harassment and economic deprivation, young Tamils are ready to give up their lives', *Far Eastern Economic Review*, 1 June:64–67.

Kaplan, A. (1981) 'The psychodynamics of terrorism', in Y. Alexander and J. Gleason (eds), *Behavioural and Quantitative Perspectives on Terrorism*, New York: Pergamon, pp. 35–510.

Kelly, R.C. (2000) *Warless Societies and the Origin of War*, Ann Arbor: The University of Michigan Press.

Khawaja, Marwan (1993) 'Repressive and popular collective action: Evidence for the West Bank', *Sociological Forum*, 8(1):47–71.

—— (1994) 'Resource mobilization, hardship, and popular collective action in the West Bank', *Social Forces*, 73(1):191–220.

Khosrokhavar, F. (2005) *Suicide Bombers: Allah's New Martyrs*, trans. from French by David Macey, London: Pluto Press.

Kim, S. and Smith, R. (1993) 'Revenge and conflict escalation', *Negotiation Journal*, 9:37–43.

Kobrin, N. Hartevelt (2002) 'A psychoanalytic approach to bin Laden, political, domestic violence and Islamic suicide terrorism', in Orbach (2004).

Kozu, N. (2000) 'Human torpedo', in Haruko Cook and Theodore Cook (eds), *Japan at War: An Oral History*, London: Phoenix Press.

Kramer, Martin (1991) 'Sacrifice and "self-martyrdom" in Shi'ite Lebanon', *Terrorism and Political Violence*, 3(3):30–47.

Krueger, A.B. and Maleckova, J. (2003) 'Education, poverty and terrorism: Is there a causal connection?', *Journal of Economic Perspectives*, 17(4):119–44.

Kubler-Ross, E. (1969) *On Death and Dying*, New York: Macmillan.

Larteguy, Jean (1956) *The Sun Goes Down: Last Letters from Japanese Suicide-Pilots and Soldiers*, London: W. Kimber.

Leenars, A. (2004) 'Altruistic suicide: A few reflections', *Archives of Suicide Research*, 81:1–7.

Lester, David, Yang, Bijou and Lindsay, Mark (2004) 'Suicide bombers: Are psychological profiles possible?', *Studies in Conflict and Terrorism*, 27(4):283–94.

Lewis, Bernard (1986) *Semites and Anti-Semites: An Inquiry into Conflict and Prejudice*, London: Weidenfeld & Nicolson.

—— (1987) *The Assassins: A Radical Sect in Islam*, New York: Oxford University Press.

Lukes, S. (1997) 'Humiliation and the politics of identity', *Social Research*, 64(1):36–51.

MacDonald, Edwina and Williams, George (2007) 'Banned books and seditious speech: Anti-terrorism laws and other threats to academic freedom', *Australia and New Zealand Journal of Law and Education*, 12(1):29–46.

Makki, Mahmoud (1992) 'The political history of Al-Andalus (92/711–897/1492)', in Jayyusi(1992), pp. 3–87.

Maleckova, Jitka (2005) 'Improvised terrorists: Stereotype or reality', in T. Bjorgo (ed.), *Root Causes of Terrorism: Myths, Reality and Ways Forward*, London: Routledge, pp. 33–43.

Margalit, Avishai (1996) *The Decent Society*, Cambridge, MA: Harvard University Press.

—— (2003) 'The suicide bombers', *New York Review of Books*, 16 January, www.nybooks.com/articles/15979.

Marzuk, P.M., Tardiff, K. and Hirsch, C.S. (1992) 'The epidemiology of murder-suicide', *JAMA*, 267:3179–83.

Menocal, Maria Roza (2002) *The Ornament of the World: How Muslims, Jews and Christians Created a Culture of Tolerance in Medieval Spain*, New York: Little, Brown.

Merari, A. (1990) 'The readiness to kill and die: Suicide terrorism in the Middle East', in W. Reich (ed.), *Origins of Terrorism*, New York: Cambridge University Press, p. 192–210.

—— (2000) 'Statement before the Special Oversight Panel on Terrorism: Terrorism and the threats to US interests in the Middle East', [HASC No. 106–59] Washington, DC: US Congress.

—— (2005a) 'Social organizational and psychological factors in suicide terrorism', in T. Bjorgo (ed.), *Root Causes of Terrorism: Myths, Reality and Ways Forward*, London: Routledge, pp. 70–86.

—— (2005b) 'Suicidal terrorism', in R.I. Yufit and D. Lester (eds), *Assessment, Treatment, and Prevention of Suicidal Behaviour*, Hoboken, NJ: Wiley.

Miller, W. (1993) *Humiliation: and Other Essays on Honor, Social Discomfort, and Violence*, Ithaca, NY: Cornell University Press.

Minois, Georges (1999) *History of Suicide: Voluntary Death in Western Culture*, Baltimore: The Johns Hopkins University Press. MIPT Terrorism Knowledge Base, http://www.tkb.org (accessed July 2005).

Moghadam, Assaf (2003) 'Palestinian suicide terrorism in the Second Intifada: Motivations and organisational aspects', *Studies in Conflict and Terrorism*, 26(2):65–92.

—— (2006) 'Suicide terrorism, occupation, and the globalization of martyrdom: A critique of *Dying to Win*', *Studies in Conflict and Terrorism*, 29(6), fletcher.tufts.edu/jebsencenter/pubs/moghadam/SCT%20Article.pdf.

—— (2008) *The Globalization of Martyrdom: Al Qaeda, Salafi Jihad, and the Diffusion of Suicide Attacks*, Baltimore: The Johns Hopkins University Press.

Nordstrom, Carolyn (1994) *Warzones: Cultures of Violence, Militarisation and Peace*, Working Paper No. 145, Peace Research Centre, Australian National University, Canberra.

—— (2004) *Shadows of War: Violence, Power, and International Profiteering in the Twenty-First Century*, Berkeley: University of California Press.

O'Donovan, Oliver (2003) *The Just War Revisited*, Cambridge: Cambridge University Press.

Oknuki-Tierney, E. (2002) *Kamikaze, Cherry Blossoms and Nationalisms: The Militarization of Aesthetics in Japanese History*, Chicago: Chicago University Press.

Oliver, Anne M. and Steinberg, Paul F. (2005) *The Road to Martyr's Square: A Journey into the World of the Suicide Bomber*, New York: Oxford University Press.

O'Neill, Margot (2006) 'Terror research under threat from Aust law', *Lateline*, 11 September, www.abc.net.au/lateline/content/2006/s1738491.htm.

O'Neill, R. (1999) *Suicide Squads*, London: Salamander Books.

Oppel, Richard A. Jr. (2007) 'Foreign fighters in Iraq are tied to allies of US', *New York Times*, 22 November.

Orbach, Israel (2004) 'Terror suicide: How is it possible?', *Archives of Suicide Research*, 8:115–30.

Otterbein, K.F. (1970) *The Evolution of War: A Cross Cultural Study*, New Haven: HRAF Press.

—— (1986) *The Ultimate Coercive Sanction*, New Haven: HRAF Press.

Pape, Robert A. (2005) *Dying to Win: The Strategic Logic of Suicide Terrorism*, New York: Random House.

Paz, Reuven (2002) 'The Islamic legitimacy of suicide terrorism', in *Countering Terrorism*, Herzliya, Israel: International Policy Institute for Counter Terrorism.

Pearlstein, R.M. (1991) *The Mind of the Political Terrorist*, Wilmington, DE: Scholarly Resources.

Pedahzur, Ami (2005) *Suicide Terrorism*, London: Polity Press.

Pedahzur, Ami and Perliger, Arie (2006) 'The changing nature of suicide attacks: A social network approach', *Social Forces*, 84(4):1988–2008.

Pedahzur, Ami, Perliger, A. and Weinberg, L. (2003) 'Altruism and fatalism: The characteristics of Palestinian suicide terrorists', *Deviant Behaviour: An Interdisciplinary Journal*, 24(4):405–23.

Physicians for Human Rights (2005) *Break Them Down: Systematic Use of Psychological Torture by US Forces*, Washington, DC: Physicians for Human Rights.

Porath, Y. (1977) *The Palestinian Arab National Movement: From Riots to Rebellion*, London: I.B.Tauris.

Post, Jerrold M. (1986) 'Hostility, conformity, fraternity: The group dynamics of terrorist behaviour', *International Journal of Group Psychotherapy*, 36:211–24.

Post, Jerrold and Denny, L. (2002) 'The terrorists in their own words', paper presented at the International Society of Political Psychology Conference, 16–19 July, Berlin.

Post, Jerrold, Sprinzak, Ehud and Denny, Laurita M. (2003) 'The terrorists in their own words: Interviews with 35 incarcerated Middle Eastern terrorists', *Terrorism and Political Violence*, 15(1):171–84.

Rapoport, David (1984) 'Fear and trembling: Terrorism in three religious traditions', *American Political Science Review*, 78(3):658–77.

—— (2002) 'Four waves of rebel terror and September 11', *Anthropoetics*, 8(1), www.anthropoetics.ucla.edu/ap0801/terror.htm (accessed1 April 2009).

Rashid, Ahmad (2001) *Taliban: The Story of the Afghan Warlords*, London: Pan Macmillan.

—— (2008a) *Descent into Chaos: The United States and the Future of Nation Building in Pakistan, Afghanistan and Central Asia*, London: Allan Lane.

—— (2008b) 'Jihadi suicide bombers: The new wave', *New York Review of Books*, 55(10), www.nybooks.com/articles/21473 (accessed 1 April 2009).

Regan, T. (2005) 'Studies: War radicalised most foreign fighters', *The Christian Science Monitor*, 18 July.

Reuter, C. (2004) *My Life is a Weapon: A Modern History of Suicide Bombings*, Princeton: Princeton University Press.

Ricolfi, L. (2005) 'Palestinians, 1981–2003', in D. Gambetta (ed.), *Making Sense of Suicide Missions*, Oxford: Oxford University Press, pp. 77–130.

Roberts, M. (2005) 'Saivite symbols, sacrifice and Tamil Tigers rites', *Social Analysis*, 49(1):67–93.

—— (2007) 'Blunders in Tigerland: Pape's Muddles on "Suicide Bombers" in Sri Lanka', Working Paper No. 32, South Asia Institute, Department of Political Science, University of Heidelberg.

—— (2008) 'Tamil Tigers: Sacrificial symbolism and dead body politics', *Anthropology Today*, 24(3):22–23.

Roy, O. (2004) 'Globalised Islam: The Search for a New Ummah', New York: Columbia University Press.

Sageman, Marc (2004) *Understanding Terror Networks*, Philadelphia: University of Pennsylvania Press.

Said, Edward (1980) *The Question of Palestine*, London: Routledge & Kegan Paul.

Saikal, Amin (2004) *Modern Afghanistan: A History of Struggle and Survival*, London: I.B.Tauris.

Saurette, Paul (2006) 'You dissin me? Humiliation and post 9/11 global politics', *Review of International Studies*, 32(3):495–522.

Sayre, Edward (2009) 'Labour market conditions, political events, and Palestinian suicide bombings', *Peace Economics, Peace Science and Public Policy*, 15(1), www. bepress. com/peps/vol15/iss1/1.

Schalk, Peter (1997a) 'Resistance and martyrdom in the process of state formation in Tamililam', in J. Pettigrew (ed.), *Martyrdom and Political Resistance: Essays from Asia and Europe*, Amsterdam: VU University Press.

—— (1997b) 'The revival of martyr cults among Ilavar', *Temenos*, 33:151–90.

Schweitzer, Y. (2007) 'Palestinian female suicide bombers: Reality and myth', in Y. Schweitzer (ed.), *Female Suicide Bombers: Dying for Equality*, Tel Aviv: Jaffee Center for Strategic Studies.

Shay, Shaul (2004) *The Shahids: Islam and Suicide Attacks*, New Brunswick: Transactions.

Shepherd, J. (2006) 'Just who is listening in?' The Times Higher Education Supplement, at www.timeshighereducation.co.uk/storyCode=206528&setioncode=26 (accessed 1 April 2009).

Shermer, M. (2006). 'Murdercide: Science Unravels the Myth of Suicide Bombers', *Scientific American*, January.

Silke, Andrew (2003) 'The psychology of suicide terrorism', in Andrew Silke (ed.), *Terrorists, Victims and Society: Psychological Perspectives on Terrorism and its Consequences*, Chichester: Wiley.

—— (2006) 'The Role of Suicide in Politics, Conflict and terrorism', *Terrorism and Political Violence*, 18(1)35–46.

—— (2007a) 'Holy warriors: Exploring the psychological processes of jihadi radicalization', *European Journal of Criminology*, 5(1):99–123.

—— (2007b) 'The role of suicide in terrorism', unpublished paper, School of Law, University of East London.

Somasundaram, Daya (ed.) (1998) *Scarred Minds: The Psychological Impact of War on Sri Lankan Tamils*, New Delhi: Sage.

—— (2008a) 'Ethnic Consciousness', unpublished paper, Department of Psychiatry, University of Adelaide.

—— (2008b) 'Parallel government: Living between terror and counter-terror in Jaffna (1982–2006)', paper presented at the Globalizing Religions Conference, University of Adelaide, 1–6 December.

—— (2010) 'Suicide bombers in Sri Lanka', *Asian Journal of Social Science*, 38(3):414–39.

Speckhard, Anne and Ahkmedova, Khapta (2006) 'The making of a martyr: Chechen suicide terrorism', *Studies in Conflict and Terrorism*, 29(5): 429–92.

Stein, R. (2002) 'Evil as love and as liberation', *Psychoanalytic Dialogue*, 12(3): 393–420.

Strenski, Ivan (2003) 'Sacrifice, gift and the social logic of Muslim human bombers', *Terrorism and Political Violence*, 15(3):1–34.

Tarrow, S. (1998) *Power in Movement: Social Movements and Contentious Politics*, Cambridge: Cambridge University Press.

Timmermans, S. (2005) 'Death brokering: constructing culturally appropriate deaths', *Sociology of Health and Illness*, 27(7):993–1013.

Townsend, E. (2007) 'Suicide terrorists: Are they suicidal?', *Suicide and Life Threatening Behaviour*, 37(1):35–49.

Trawick, M. (2007) *Enemy Lines: Warfare, Childhood, and Play in Batticaloa*, Berkeley: University of California Press.

Tuck, Richard (1999) *The Rights of War and Peace: Political Thoughts and International Order from Grotius to Kant*, Oxford: Oxford University Press.

Victor, B. (2003) 'Army of Roses: Inside the World of Palestinian Women Suicide Bombers', Emmaus, PA: Rodale.

Victoroff, J. (2005) 'The mind of the terrorist: A review and critique of psychological approaches', *Journal of Conflict Resolution*, 49(1):3–42.
Walzer, Michael (1965) *The Revolution of the Saints: A Study in the Origins of Radical Politics*, Cambridge, MA: Harvard University Press.
—— (2004) *Arguing about War*, New Haven, CT: Yale University Press.
—— (2006) 'The ethics of battle: War fair', *The New Republic*, 31 July:15–16.
Weiss, M. (2006) *Protest and Possibilities: Civil Society and Coalitions for Political Change in Malaysia*, Stanford: Stanford University Press.
Wright, Q. (1942) *A Study of War*, Chicago: University of Chicago Press.
Zimbardo, P. (2007) *The Lucifer Effect*, New York: The Random House.

INDEX

Page numbers in *italics* denote a figure/table